Desserts 1-2-3

ALSO BY ROZANNE GOLD

Little Meals

Recipes 1-2-3

Recipes 1-2-3 Menu Cookbook

Entertaining 1-2-3

Healthy 1-2-3

Desserts 1-2-3

Deliciously Simple Three-Ingredient Recipes

Rozanne Gold

Photographs by Judd Pilossof

Stewart, Tabori & Chang
New York

**This book is dedicated to
my beautiful mother, Marion, and my generous father, Bill.**

Text copyright © 2002 Rozanne Gold

Photographs copyright © 2002 Judd Pilossof, except for the photographs on pages 5, 12, 37, 68, 83, 109, 117, 123, and endpapers

Food styling by Elizabeth Duffy

Design by Amanda Wilson Design, Inc.

Published in 2002 by

Stewart, Tabori & Chang

A Company of La Martinière Groupe

115 West 18th Street

New York, NY 10011

Export sales to all countries except Canada, France,

and French-speaking Switzerland:

Thames and Hudson Ltd.

181A High Holborn

London WC1V 7QX

England

Canadian Distribution:

Canadian Manda Group

One Atlantic Avenue, Suite 105

Toronto, Ontario M6K 3E7

Canada

Library of Congress Cataloging-in-Publication Data

Gold, Rozanne,1954-
    Desserts 1-2-3 ; deliciously simple three-ingredient recipes / by Rozanne Gold ;
  photographs by Judd Pilossof.
       p. cm.
     Includes index.
     ISBN 1-58479-099-7
      1. Desserts. 2. Quick and easy cookery. I. Title: Desserts one, two, three. II. Title.

  TX773 .G55 2002
  641.8'6--dc21

                                                                    2001058526

The text of this book was composed in Akzidenz Grotesk.

Printed in Singapore

10 9 8 7 6 5 4 3 2 1

First Printing

contents

Desserts 1-2-3

Pablo Neruda wrote odes to life;
To nature, to love, to the sun,

I prefer writing odes to sweets,
and worship them one by one.

Crème brûlée takes your breath away
when it shatters the quiet below,

And chocolate soufflé topped with chocolate sorbet
can sweeten most any woe.

In happier days, à la mode was the vogue
and crowned many an apple pie,

But today it is sleek, and undoubtedly chic,
to find them side by side.

For some of you chocolate gives meaning to life,
for others it merely suffices.

Whether a pro or a rookie, in a truffle or cookie,
chocolate is great in a crisis.

"Simple pleasures are life's greatest treasures,"
Neruda once whispered to me.

He then kissed my hand and gave me a pan,
and slowly counted to three.

Rozanne Gold
Park Slope, Brooklyn, October 2001

Acknowledgments

SHORT AND SWEET SEEMS TO BE THE RIGHT APPROACH FOR THANKING THOSE WHO HELPED ME create a very delicious book. In that spirit I thank my husband, Michael Whiteman, whose intelligence is as addictive as chocolate, whose wit is a web of spun sugar and spice, whose honesty and integrity could soften a rock-solid pint of Häagen-Dasz. He is as unassuming as a baked apple, elegant as a soufflé. When life is bittersweet, he makes me a cup of tea with a smile that makes lemon drops melt.

My publisher, Leslie Stoker, is smooth as crème brûlée, cool as double-raspberry sorbet, and smart as they come. Her commitment to beauty and quality is matched only by her respect for equality. I have adored working with her as much as I adore Roasted Strawberry Ice Cream with Fresh Strawberry Compote.

Jack Lamplough, Director of Publicity at STC, is nothing short of Chocolate Delicato: rich with kindness and unexpected diplomacy.

Paige Sarlin, our administrative assistant, has brought sweetness and light to our lives for several years. A fabulous artist, may she enjoy Pineapple Carpaccio with Roasted Grapes and live happily ever after.

All the cookies in this book are dedicated to Viktor Baker for leading me to the astonishing photographer Judd Pilossof. Judd made the photographs mouthwateringly scrumptious and helped me illuminate the beauty of simplicity. Liz Duffy may be the best and most talented food stylist I've ever worked with, and her assistant, Lynn Schnarr is all peaches and cream. More thanks to the J. Pilossof atelier, including Amy Thomas and Tracy Young.

Amanda Wilson, book designer extraordinaire, is as stylish as Maple Chiffon, as impressive as a Chocolate Cream and Raspberry Parfait. Her aesthetic sense has enlightened my own sense of taste.

A special thanks to Tom Eckerle, who shot the "1-2-3 cookies" used as endpapers in this book. And kisses to Jerry Ruotolo, who provided the lovely image of my Melon Tartare with Raspberries.

Helen Kimmel, MS, RD, has been along for the culinary journey throughout the 1-2-3 series. Her talents are many, and she has lovingly and professionally analyzed over seven hundred recipes since we've started. She can be any dessert she wants to be.

Then there are my friends—as enriching as Chocolate Demitasse with Soft Whipped Cream, as nurturing as Warm Plums in Ruby Syrup. They know who they are and what they mean to me; they've been listed by name in each of my other books. A lifetime supply of Chocolate-Pepper Truffles goes to my very smart brother, Leon, and his wife, Gail.

And here's to my son, Jeremy Whiteman, the crème de la crème.

Desserts 1-2-3 is the sweet finale to my three-ingredient cookbook series. It is the end of a serendipitous culinary journey that has allowed me to explore the essences of cooking and baking, to appreciate the beauty of restraint, and to respect the untrammeled flavors of the best ingredients.

My search for simplicity has been a delicious one, but never more so than in the creation of an entire book devoted to desserts. It has been especially enlightening because I am not a born baker or pastry chef. Each recipe was the result of trial and error, repetition, frustration, then finally delight. Professional chefs tend to specialize in one area, and my specialty has never been sweets. But I found that it's never too late to develop a passion.

One can wax rhapsodic about the way dark chocolate mousse lightly floats on the tongue, or wonder how Lemon Melting Moments tastes like frozen sunshine, or remark about the improbability of a three-ingredient cake, or marvel at how strawberries, sugar, and wonton wrappers can become three desserts in one. You'll probably want to see for yourself.

Nowhere is the expression "the proof of the pudding is in the eating" more apt than in creating dessert extravaganzas with just three ingredients. I offer you more than 130 recipes, including fresh fruit desserts, custards, soufflés, cakes, tarts, chocolate desserts, and ice creams, and there are 100 "ideas" that dramatically illuminate the simple philosophy of *Desserts 1-2-3*: easy to make, great to look at, decadent to eat.

Desserts are designed to tease. They are the ultimate temptation when one's appetite has largely been satisfied. And although the word dessert (from the French word *desservir*, meaning to remove the dishes or clear the table) refers to any sweet dish considered suitable for the last course of a meal, the qualities that make a perfect dessert are highly subjective. For some it might mean something light and refreshing, such as my Strawberry-Lemongrass Consommé with Cut Berries; for others, a thoughtful pairing of fruit and cheese would be sublime; and many would treasure a scoop of intensely flavored fruit sorbet accompanied by a delicate cookie. For hedonists, if it isn't chocolate, it isn't dessert.

Naturally, these desserts are not meant solely for the end of a meal, but will be welcome almost any time of the day.

ABOUT THE RECIPES AND INGREDIENTS

Some desserts are homey and comforting, many are sleek and contemporary, some are fun and fanciful, others luxuriously rich. I have grouped them according to style: brilliant fresh fruits in season; things that wobble, like custards and soufflés; baked goods—cakes, cookies, tarts; chocolate in all forms; and frozen desserts—ices, granitas, sorbets, semifreddos, and ice creams.

As with all the books in my 1-2-3 series, every recipe uses only three ingredients (not including salt, pepper, and water, which I consider "free" ingredients). You may be surprised to learn that salt is an integral part of baking and dessert making. A pinch of salt helps egg whites stiffen, and salt actually can accentuate or balance the taste of sugar in a recipe. Coarsely ground white pepper adds a grace note to my Nectarine Tower with Honey-Glazed Wontons, while freshly ground black pepper adds verve and authenticity to sinful Chocolate-Pepper Truffles (the Mexicans, Spanish, and even the French used to add chile to their chocolate in the eighteenth century).

The inspiration for most of the recipes came from the main ingredient—perfectly ripe berries, apples from a local orchard, a block of super-premium chocolate—which is always sweetened, but not in obvious ways. Naturally, sugar is used often, and the many different types of sugar add their own nuances and colors to a dish. There is familiar granulated sugar and confectioners' sugar, but also turbinado sugar, pearl sugar, dark brown sugar, pellets of rock sugar, and rainbow-colored crystals (which come in purple, red, orange, yellow, and even black). Other sweeteners include aromatic honeys, maple syrup, reductions of pineapple juice, and apple cider. Two indispensable sweeteners are vanilla-sugar and cinnamon-sugar, which you can buy, but are easy to make yourself. They are my only two essential pantry staples and I suggest you prepare them in large quantity since they last indefinitely and you'll use them often. (See page 11.)

For more detailed information about chocolate, turn to the chapter that begins on page 119. Although everyone has their own chocolate preferences, in general, the better the chocolate, the more compelling the result; and the less sweet the chocolate, the deeper the flavor.

I always use extra-large eggs and unsalted butter.

My 1-2-3 dessert pantry also includes good-quality cocoa powder; cream of coconut for making coconut custard and coconut sorbet; sweetened condensed milk for pecan bars and *dolce de leche*; Nutella (chocolate-hazelnut spread) for making cookies and for mixing with yogurt to make a dip for fresh figs; halvah for shaving onto fresh pears and also for making cookies; almond syrup (also known as orgeat or orzata) for making ices and granitas; imported raspberry preserves for a last-minute soufflé, and blocks of premium bittersweet chocolate and bags of chocolate chips for baking brownies, churning sorbet, and making rich chocolate pudding to eat right out of the pot.

NUTRITIONALLY SPEAKING

Almost one-third of these scrumptious recipes are fat free and/or low calorie (see page 169). Fat free means just that; low calorie means 165 or fewer calories per serving. That's less than a container of yogurt! Helen Kimmel, MS, RD, who has masterfully done the nutritional analyses for all of my books, was especially delighted with these outcomes. It's hard to imagine that Poached Pineapple in Lemon Syrup with Pineapple Granita and Pineapple Chips is a fat-free offering, and that Ultra-Light Brownies made with real

chocolate, eggs, and sugar is low calorie, but here they are. As for the other recipes, according to Helen, "there are beneficial nutrients in all natural, unprocessed foods, so don't deprive yourself of any of these ultra-satisfying recipes. If you're dieting, just eat smaller servings."

KEEP-IT-SIMPLE EQUIPMENT

Since dessert making and baking is a rather new pastime for me, I do not own fancy pans, or candy thermometers, or silicon mats (known professionally as Silpat). I do, however, have a standing mixer (with two bowls so I don't have to wash a bowl before advancing to another step in a recipe), a few sheet pans, one cookie pan, spatulas and knives, 9-inch and 10-inch springform pans, and removable-bottom tart pans in several shapes and sizes. I use parchment paper and nonstick vegetable cooking spray and have two cherished rolling pins—one from my great-grandmother Rose, and one from my mother-in-law, Anne Frieda. A double boiler is essential for many of these recipes, but you can fashion your own by placing a metal bowl on a pot of simmering water so that it sits comfortably above but not touching the water. Have a wire rack on hand for cooling cakes and cookies.

Other essentials, which you should have in your kitchen anyway, include a digital scale, measuring cups and spoons, an oven thermometer, a few pastry brushes, and a flexible rubber spatula. Nonessentials include an offset spatula, a citrus zester (although the small holes of a box grater will do), and a pastry bag with large tips for piping meringue (but you can make lovely designs using a spoon). And there are those cute little blowtorches, available in many cookware shops for caramelizing sugar for beloved crème brûlée, but that can be done in your broiler. For information on ice cream makers, see chapter 6.

If having the right equipment is important, than reading a recipe thoroughly before you get started is critical: that includes having all the ingredients organized and prepped as they are called for in the recipe (in professional kitchens, this is called *mise en place*—literally, to put in place), and all equipment spanking clean and thoroughly dried.

THE BEAUTY OF SIMPLICITY

As a professional chef for over two decades, I have had the good fortune to be involved with some of the most glamorous restaurants in the country, where presentation was tantamount to taste. It was at the magical Rainbow Room and Windows on the World, now sadly gone, that I learned little tricks for making chocolate curls and piping meringue and spinning candy from caramelized sugar. I don't do these things with great skill, but have tried to share some of these techniques with you.

You will notice from the striking photographs and the detailed instructions for presenting these desserts that they require little embellishment. The real creativity, and fun, comes from using one ingredient in several different ways. For example, the "insignia" on the baked apples (page 50) is nothing more than cinnamon-sugar that has been melted to liquid form and then squiggled on to foil until it hardens. Pecan-Fudge Terrine (page 139) is adorned with an edible garnish of pecan halves, half-dipped in chocolate. Candied citrus rinds dress up several of their respective fruit desserts.

Following, as I always do, the less-is-more style of visual harmony, I usually leave well enough alone.

ONE BIG DESSERT PARTY

One thinks of cocktail parties, buffets, and sit-down dinners when one thinks of entertaining. But I love a parade of desserts. The idea is a nod to France, where, according to *The Oxford Companion to Food*, during the early to mid-eighteenth century the "dessert comprised impressive pyramids of fruit and sweetmeats, displayed in rococo style on tables decorated with flowers and tall candelabra." In 1861 the American Mrs. Beeton retaliated with "choice and delicately flavored cakes and biscuits, served with most costly and recherché wines, plus candied fruits and other morsels such as chocolate." And it's all here in *Desserts 1-2-3*. Since it's 2002 and you're not sure where (or what) your candelabrum is, keep it simple and throw one big dessert party for fun.

However, during a more formal sit-down dinner, I like to break with tradition. Sometimes I serve dessert in two courses, first a sorbet, followed by a cake. Other times, I make two contrasting but compatible desserts and give one to the men and one to the women. Or I serve each guest tiny portions of three desserts on a large dinner plate. Often, fruit and cheese becomes the dessert course, followed by an extravagant dessert wine or brandy.

I always give my guests something sweet to take home. For this purpose, you have miraculous three-ingredient cookie recipes from which to choose (pages 108–116).

WHAT TO DRINK?

When it comes to dessert, pairing food and wine can be particularly challenging, but there are simple rules to follow. The wine should be sweeter than the dessert (or the wine will taste tinny and thin); and the wine and dessert should have a similar "weight" or body (a full-bodied wine will overwhelm a light, delicate dessert; a rich, creamy dessert will conquer a light-bodied wine).

A wine should complement the dessert's inherent flavors. Some examples: chocolate desserts partner well with ruby port or Madeira; fresh fruit desserts are enhanced by late-harvest Rieslings, ice wines, Hungarian Tokay, and Moscato d'Asti; desserts featuring nuts and dried fruit go beautifully with oloroso and cream sherries, Bual or Malmsey Madeiras; custards and creamy desserts marry well with Monbazillac or Barsac from France and sweet Malvasia from Italy; cookies go well with vin santo for dunking (and are also excellent with milk).

Some sweet wines are so distinctive and full-bodied that they become desserts in themselves, especially German Trockenbeerenausleses and leggy French Sauternes. An older off-dry champagne from a great producer can also stand alone. I don't understand why some foodies serve very dry, expensive champagne with dessert when an off-dry or even sweet bubbly is far more appropriate. And there's nothing wrong with resurrecting that old standby, Asti Spumante.

Fruit and cheese become cause for celebration when paired with wine. These are the discoveries you make yourself—be sure to write them down for future reference. Some combinations I adore include Jurançon with Gorgonzola; Sauternes with Roquefort; Australian semchard with a slightly aged goat cheese; oloroso sherry with manchego; slightly sweet Gewürztraminer with real Muenster cheese; and classic Stilton with port. Liqueurs and spirits can also complement many desserts. Single-malt Scotch and single-barrel bourbons go well with chocolate and coffee desserts; a splash of cassis in a glass of bubbly is a great accompaniment to fresh fruit tarts; Calvados goes hand in hand with apple desserts and is especially delicious with my Sweet Apple Frittata; a snifter of Poire Williams is heavenly with pastry-wrapped pear Bourdelots; a shot of Kahlúa in steamed milk tastes great with a plate of brownies; a pony glass of framboise is elegant alongside Warm Raspberry Soufflé; amaretto tastes yummy with orange-based desserts; and a good old-fashioned "grasshopper" (green crème de menthe, crème de cocoa, and heavy cream) tastes awesome with a slice of Michael's Chocolate Obsession.

In Europe, coffee or espresso is always served after dessert; in America it is generally served with dessert. The choice is up to you.

The evocative food writer Laurie Colwin once wrote that "it sometimes seems as though the world is divided into those who are waiting for dessert and those who have to produce it." My hope is that *Desserts 1-2-3* brings special gratification to both.

TWO BASIC RECIPES

Don't even think of getting started on the recipes in this book without having a supply of vanilla-sugar and cinnamon-sugar in your pantry. You can buy these staples, but it is far more economical to make them.

Vanilla-Sugar

4 cups granulated sugar
2 long moist vanilla beans

Put sugar in a medium bowl. Place vanilla beans on a cutting board and cut beans in half lengthwise. With the tip of a small knife, scrape out the seeds and add them to the sugar, using your fingers to incorporate them. Transfer sugar to a jar or container with a tight-fitting cover. Stick halved vanilla beans deep into the sugar and cover tightly. Lasts indefinitely.

Makes 4 cups

Cinnamon-Sugar

2 cups granulated sugar
3 tablespoons good-quality ground cinnamon

Place sugar in a small bowl. Stir in cinnamon and mix thoroughly. Transfer to a jar or container with a tight-fitting cover. Lasts indefinitely.

Makes 2 cups

Fresh Fruit Desserts

SEVERAL YEARS AGO AT A NONDESCRIPT BREAKFAST BUFFET IN SOUTHERN CALIFORNIA,
I sleepily put some fresh fruit on my plate. Looking down at the haphazard arrangement, I was awestruck by the simplicity and majesty before me. A few slices of garnet watermelon with ebony seeds, an arc of pale jade honeydew, a golden tranche of pineapple. Perhaps it was the California sun that made the colors of these three fruits so electrifying, or the juxtaposition of shapes against a translucent white background, but at that moment I reveled in the sheer opulence of God's color scheme.

A Japanese proverb states that "if you can capture the season on a plate, then you are the master." This is the intention of this chapter: to inspire you, when you go to your local market, farm stand, or supermarket produce section, to joyfully prepare the brilliant array that lies before you.

Here are more than thirty-five desserts featuring twenty fresh fruits—from the first strawberries and rhubarb in spring, all manner of berries and stone fruits in summer, apples and sweet pears in the fall, to myriad citrus in winter. Even though the concept of seasonality shifts as the availability of fruits from other countries widens, you have no doubt experienced the pure pleasure of a juicy peach, a succulent fig, or the perfume of a perfectly ripe melon—each in its own local season. Inferior fruit can undo the essence of these recipes.

You will enjoy the variety of desserts you can make from a single fruit. For example, ripe strawberries can be cooked to a flavorful compote laced with cinnamon-sugar and topped with a timbale of melting yogurt, or they can be fashioned into a modern consommé perfumed with lemongrass. Pineapple? There are sculpted wedges poached in lemon syrup and thick rings slowly cooked in pure maple syrup and strewn with toasted sesame seeds.

For those who crave cheese, as I do, there are fruit-and-cheese trios that become "dessert" when thoughtfully combined—fleshy figs and ricotta with a honey-fig coulis, and roasted grapes and Asian pears with Gorgonzola and fresh grape syrup.

What to drink? Off-dry sparkling wines go beautifully with many fruit desserts, as do Sauternes, ice wine, white port, sweeter-style sherries, and many German Ausleses, and Austrian Rieslings.

Strawberry-Cinnamon Compote with Frozen Yogurt Timbale

20 ounces vanilla yogurt

1¼ pounds large ripe strawberries

¼ cup cinnamon-sugar, plus additional for garnish

This is a dessert to cool you down in summer and comfort you in winter. Sweetly spiced fruit, warm and yielding, comes alive under a slowly melting igloo of tangy yogurt. Focus on the interplay of texture, taste, and temperature.

Drain yogurt and distribute equally among four decorative 5-ounce molds or timbales. Place in freezer for 2 hours or until frozen.

Save 4 small strawberries for garnish. Remove stems from remaining strawberries and wash.

Shake off water. Place strawberries in a saucepan with cinnamon-sugar. Let sit 30 minutes. Some liquid will seep from the berries. Bring contents to a boil. Lower heat to medium and cook 10 to 15 minutes, until strawberries are soft but still retain their shape. Sauce should be thick. Let cool. Distribute strawberries and sauce among 4 bowls. Strawberries and sauce should be slightly warm or at room temperature.

Unmold frozen yogurt and place on top of strawberries. Thinly slice reserved strawberries, leaving stem end intact; fan out the sliced strawberries and place over the yogurt molds. If desired, sprinkle edge of bowls with cinnamon-sugar.

Serves 4

Strawberry-Lemongrass Consommé with Cut Berries

6 stalks lemongrass

2 pints ripe strawberries

⅔ cup sugar or vanilla-sugar

Blades of once-exotic lemongrass, a staple of Thai cuisine, now can be found in many supermarkets' produce sections (next to the kaffir lime leaves and galanga). Lemongrass has a haunting lemon-lime flavor that, in combination with sweet-scented strawberries, will fill your nostrils with an alluring perfume. My husband often tosses a spoonful of wine into warm, savory soups, a trick he picked up in France. This bonne idée works equally well with cold soups: add a splash of white port, moscato, Japanese plum wine, or even sweet vermouth to a sweet soup like this one and to hell with restraint!

Split lemongrass stalks in half lengthwise and remove the tender core toward the bottom of the blade. Mince the tender core finely. Using a sharp knife, coarsely chop the outer core of the lemongrass stalks so that you have ⅓ cup. Place in a saucepan.

Finely chop enough strawberries to get ½ cup. Add to saucepan with 4 cups water, ⅔ cup sugar, and 8 black peppercorns. Bring to a boil. Lower heat and simmer 20 minutes.

Pour through a fine-mesh sieve and return liquid to saucepan over medium-high heat. Cook until liquid is reduced to 2¾ cups. Chill until very cold.

Wash remaining berries, saving 2 medium berries, with stems, for garnish. Thinly slice half of the berries lengthwise; dice remaining berries into small cubes. Arrange an assortment of berry shapes in the bottom of 4 large flat soup plates. Place a halved berry with stem in center. Pour chilled broth evenly over berries. (Or present bowls of berries without the broth. Then ladle the liquid from a pretty glass bowl over the berries in front of your guests.)

Serves 4

Sautéed Strawberries in Lemon Oil, Strawberry Sorbetto

5 pints ripe strawberries

¾ cup sugar

1 tablespoon plus 2 teaspoons lemon olive oil

Here's a demure dish that sings with flavor. It's especially fragrant during the summer months, but enjoyable all year long. Natural pectin in the strawberries allows the fruit juices to thicken at room temperature, and a small amount of lemon-scented olive oil adds a creamy, rich mouthfeel while still maintaining this dessert's low-fat credentials.

TO MAKE THE SORBETTO: Wash and dry 2 pints of strawberries. Remove stems. Puree in a food processor with 1 cup water and ½ cup sugar. Process until smooth, then strain through a sieve into a bowl. Chill mixture. Freeze in an ice cream machine according to the manufacturer's directions.

At least 30 minutes before serving, wash and dry remaining 3 pints strawberries. Save 6 small strawberries with stems for garnish. Cut remaining strawberries into small cubes. Heat the oil in a large nonstick skillet. Add the cubed berries with ¼ cup sugar. Cook over high heat 2 minutes, or until strawberries are soft but still retain their shape. Cool to room temperature.

When ready to serve, spoon strawberries and their sauce into 6 flat-rimmed soup plates or wine glasses. Top each with a scoop of sorbet. Garnish each serving with a small whole strawberry.

Serves 6

Rhubarb Compote
with Candied Ginger, Maple Snow

1½ cups pure maple syrup

2 pounds rhubarb

⅓ cup slivered candied ginger

The most surprising element of this dessert may be the maple snow, which is nothing more than maple syrup churned into a milky, sorbet-like treat. The combination of tart rhubarb cooked in more maple syrup, then showered with bits of candied ginger, is exhilarating.
The maple snow is best made in a real ice cream maker, but you can also freeze the mixture, scraping it with a fork every 30 minutes, until it becomes the next best thing—maple slush.

In a small bowl, combine ¾ cup maple syrup and 1⅛ cups water. Pour into an ice cream machine and freeze according to the manufacturer's directions, or pour into a shallow pan and place in freezer, scraping with a fork every 30 minutes to break up ice crystals, for 3 hours, or until frozen.

Trim rhubarb. Cut into 2½ inch lengths, and cut these into strips. Heat ¾ cup maple syrup in a very large nonstick skillet until hot. Add rhubarb and cook over medium heat until rhubarb is soft, about 15 minutes. Rhubarb should collapse but still retain some shape (you do not want this to have a souplike consistency). Remove from heat and stir in ¼ cup ginger. Let cool, then refrigerate until cold.

When ready to serve, spoon rhubarb into 6 dessert dishes. Top with maple snow from the ice cream machine, or process frozen maple slush from the freezer in a food processor until a smooth sorbet is formed. Garnish with remaining ginger. Serve immediately.

Serves 6

Rhubarb-Cherry Bisque with Red Cherry Syrup

2½ pounds trimmed rhubarb

1¾ pounds sweet red cherries

1¼ cups vanilla sugar

Rhubarb, a sassy harbinger of spring, traditionally is paired with the season's first strawberries. But here, this vegetable cozies up to fresh sweet cherries, first seen in the marketplace in late April and early May. (Those from Washington State are particularly delicious.) The result is a mouthwatering chilled soup so creamy that I've called it a bisque; its stunning color should be a new shade of lipstick.

Wash rhubarb and remove any stringy parts. Cut into 1-inch pieces. Place in a medium pot. Set aside 8 cherries with stems for garnish. Remove stems from remaining cherries and pit. Coarsely chop 1¼ pounds cherries and add to pot with rhubarb. (Set aside remaining cherries.) Make sure to add any accumulated juices. Add 1 cup plus 2 tablespoons vanilla sugar and 1 cup water.

Bring to a rapid boil. Lower heat and simmer 20 minutes. Let cool. Transfer to a food processor and process for several minutes, until very smooth. Cover and refrigerate several hours, until very cold. Soup will thicken considerably.

Chop remaining pitted cherries and place in a small saucepan with ½ cup water and 2 tablespoons vanilla sugar. Bring to a boil. Lower heat to medium and cook 15 minutes, stirring frequently. Place mixture in a fine-mesh sieve over a bowl and press down hard. Mash cherries through the sieve with the back of a large spoon until all the cherries have been sieved. You will have about ¾ cup syrup. Return to saucepan and cook over high heat until reduced to about ½ cup. Let cool.

Ladle soup into 8 dessert bowls or coffee cups. Drizzle each with cherry syrup. Garnish with a whole cherry with stem in center or sliver remaining cherries and scatter on soup, if desired. Serve immediately.

Serves 8

Apricot Coupe with Two Sauces

12 large apricots (about 2 pounds)

6 tablespoons confectioners' sugar

1 cup pineapple cottage cheese

Fromage blanc is a fresh white French cheese that has the consistency of pureed cottage cheese. Sometimes it is sweetened and served with cream and berries; other times it's mixed with garlic and fresh herbs and, according to Jacques Pépin, eaten as dessert. I decided to invent my own sweet version by adding confectioners' sugar to pineapple cottage cheese. The resulting sweet cheese tastes a little like ultra-creamy cheesecake. It goes extremely well with juicy, ripe apricots, here used both raw and cooked: the former simply diced; the latter whirled into a lovely second dessert sauce.

Place 6 apricots in a large saucepan with 2 cups water. Bring to a rapid boil. Cover pot and lower heat to medium. Cook 12 to 15 minutes, until apricots are soft. Remove apricots with slotted spoon and discard pits. Place in bowl of a food processor, making sure no cooking liquid is added. Add 3 tablespoons sugar and process until completely smooth and thick. Set aside.

Wash bowl of food processor and dry well. Place cottage cheese and remaining 3 tablespoons sugar in bowl and process for several minutes, until very smooth and creamy.

Cut remaining apricots into ¼-inch dice. Place sweet cheese sauce in bottoms of 4 large coupes or martini glasses, saving a little for garnish. Mound diced apricots in center. Cover with apricot sauce. Drizzle with remaining sweet cheese sauce and refrigerate. Serve very cold.

Serves 4

Upside-Down Fruit Crisp

8 large firm ripe nectarines or peaches

7 tablespoons unsalted butter

1½ cups good-quality granola

You can serve this granola-side-up for a more classic fruit crisp, but when turned out upside down, it unexpectedly resembles a classy fruit tart. Use flavorful, firm fruit because it gets cooked twice, first sautéed, then baked: The goal is to release the delicious juices while still retaining the fruit's shape. Serve slightly warm or at room temperature.

Preheat oven to 375° F.

Cut fruit in half lengthwise and remove pits. Cut each half into 3 or 4 wedges. Melt 3½ tablespoons butter in a large nonstick skillet. Add fruit wedges. Sauté over medium-high heat for about 8 minutes, until fruit is golden brown and beginning to soften.

Add 1 cup water and increase heat to high. Cook, stirring occasionally, until fruit is soft and most of the liquid has evaporated. Let cool.

In bowl of a food processor, put granola, remaining 3½ tablespoons butter cut into small pieces, and 2 tablespoons water. Process until crumbs just hold together.

Spray 4 gratin dishes, ramekins, or small shallow bowls (about 6 ounces each) with cooking spray. Pack in cooked fruit and all its juices. Distribute granola mixture evenly on top of fruit, making sure to cover completely. Pack down tightly.

Bake 20 minutes. Remove from oven and let cool 15 minutes. Carefully turn out onto 4 large plates. The best way to do this is to place a plate upside-down over the crisp. Using a kitchen towel (the dish will still be warm), turn the two over so that the plate is right side up. Remove the gratin dish. Trim the granola edges if you wish. Serve warm or at room temperature.

Serves 4

Nectarine Tower
with Honey-Glazed Wontons

16 square wonton wrappers

½ cup buckwheat honey

5 large ripe nectarines

Here, trendy (and widely available) wonton wrappers are varnished with aromatic honey and baked until crisp. Sweet summer nectarines are cut into wedges and drizzled with honey, salt, and coarsely ground white pepper. It all stacks up to a very impressive dessert that is easier to prepare than it may seem.

Preheat oven to 375°F. Place wonton wrappers on a cookie sheet. Fold 4 of the wonton wrappers over almost in half, leaving about ⅛ inch as a border (see photo). Heat ⅓ cup honey in a small saucepan until just warm. Using a pastry brush, spread honey lightly on each wonton wrapper to cover completely. Bake 5 to 6 minutes, until crisp.

Wash nectarines and dry well. Cut in half and remove pits. Cut each half into 6 wedges.

Place in a bowl. Drizzle with remaining honey. Add a pinch of salt and coarsely ground white pepper. Stir gently.

Place 1 flat wonton wrapper in the center of each of 4 plates. Add some of the nectarines. Place another flat wonton wrapper on top. Add another layer of nectarines. Add a wonton and more nectarines. Top with folded wonton wrapper. Drizzle with any remaining juices in the bowl.

You may also drizzle the plate with additional honey, if desired, and a little coarsely cracked white pepper. Serve within 1 hour.

Serves 4

Baked Stuffed Peaches with Toasted Almonds, Brown Sugar Syrup

**½ cup shelled whole almonds
with skins**

½ cup dark brown sugar

5 large ripe peaches

Peaches and almonds have a natural affinity. The idea here is to toast whole almonds (the skins add an extra flavor dimension) and then make a homemade almond paste to replace the pits. Extra-peachy: the warm stuffed peaches sit in a puddle of freshly made peach puree.

Preheat oven to 450°F.

Place ¼ cup sugar in a small saucepan with ¾ cup water. Bring to a boil and boil for 2 minutes. Remove syrup from heat.

Place almonds in a pie pan and bake 5 to 6 minutes, until just toasted. Let cool completely. Place in a food processor with ¼ cup sugar. Add 2 tablespoons syrup and process until a paste is formed.

Cut peaches in half and remove pits. Fill the cavities of 8 of the halves with almond paste so that it looks like you're replacing the pits. Leave 2 cavities empty. Place peach halves in a shallow casserole and pour all but 2 tablespoons syrup over peaches. Bake 10 to 12 minutes, until just tender.

Remove stuffed peaches with a slotted spoon and transfer to a platter. Spoon some of the pan juices over peaches. Cut unfilled peach halves into chunks and place in a blender or food processor with 2 tablespoons remaining syrup. Process until smooth.

Place a little of the peach puree in center of each of 4 large dessert dishes or flat soup plates. Place 2 peach halves on top. Drizzle with pan juices. Serve warm or at room temperature.

Serves 4

Sauternes-Poached Peaches à la Sabayon

4 large ripe yellow peaches

2½ cups Sauternes*

6 extra-large egg yolks

The simplest recipe for a ripe summer peach is to wash and dry it tenderly, warm it in a sunny window for 30 minutes . . . and then eat it. The most sublime recipe for a ripe summer peach is to poach it in simple syrup and add a shot of brandy. The most spectacular recipe for a ripe summer peach is the one that follows.

Wash peaches. Place in a large saucepan. Add 2 cups Sauternes and enough cold water to just cover. Bring to a boil and cook over medium-high heat about 15 minutes, until peaches are soft but still retain their shape. This will depend on the ripeness of the fruit.

Remove peaches with a slotted spoon and place in a colander to cool a bit. Cook liquid in saucepan over high heat until reduced to 1⅓ cups. Let cool.

Carefully peel peaches under cool running water. Pat dry. Place each peach in a large wine goblet. Pour ⅓ cup cooled reduced Sauternes over each peach. Keep at room temperature (or you can chill the peaches and prepare sabayon right before serving).

Put egg yolks into a large metal bowl set over a pot of simmering water. Make sure bowl does not touch the water. Whip yolks with a wire whisk, incorporating as much air as possible. Adjust the heat so that the eggs don't cook but just begin to thicken and expand. This will take about 8 minutes. Slowly add 6 to 8 tablespoons remaining Sauternes, beating constantly over medium-high heat. Continue to whisk, about 5 minutes longer, until the sabayon has tripled in volume and is the consistency of whipped cream.

Spoon sabayon over room-temperature or chilled peaches. Serve while sabayon is still warm.

Serves 4

*If you'd rather not splurge on real Sauternes, substitute another dessert wine, like Quady Essencia.

Summer Plum and Mint Compote, Almond Sorbet

½ cup plus 6 tablespoons almond syrup*

12 large ripe plums (about 2 pounds)

1 bunch spearmint

Here's how to taste this: incorporate each of the separate elements onto your spoon: fruit, syrup, mint, sorbet. Using ripe summer plums is essential, but it's the synergy of the fruit, mint, and almond essence that provides the magic.

TO MAKE SORBET: In a heavy metal pie pan, put ½ cup almond syrup and 1 cup plus 2 tablespoons cold water. Stir until completely blended. Freeze in ice cream maker or place in freezer for 3 hours, scraping with a fork every 30 minutes to break up the crystals, until it is frozen. Cover and keep in freezer.

Wash plums. Cut in half and remove stones. Cut each half into 3 wedges. Place plum wedges in a medium pot. Add 6 tablespoons almond syrup and ¼ cup cold water. Bring to a boil. Lower heat and cook over medium-high heat until plums soften but still retain their shape. Using a slotted spoon, transfer plums to a bowl. Cook juices in pan over high heat for 30 seconds. Pour over plums. Finely julienne 2 tablespoons mint and gently stir into plums. Cover and refrigerate until cold.

Place blade of food processor in freezer until cold. When ready to serve, spoon plums and juices into four or more shallow glass bowls or flat soup plates. Place sorbet in food processor and process briefly until smooth. Serve fruit with a scoop of almond sorbet and garnish with a large sprig of mint. Serve immediately.

Serves 4

*Also known as orzata or orgeat syrup, milky almond syrup is available at specialty food stores and some supermarkets.

Warm Plums in Ruby Syrup, Whipped Mascarpone

12 large ripe red plums (about 2½ pounds)

1¼ cups plus good-quality currant jelly

8 ounces mascarpone cheese

For this recipe I use plump Santa Rosa plums, one of the most popular varieties on the market. The riper they are, the more impressive their sweet contrast with tart currant jelly. The syrup is indeed ruby-colored and looks dramatic under a hillock of rich mascarpone, the Italian cheese that tiramisu made famous.

Wash plums and cut in half. Remove pits. Place plums in a medium pot and add 1 cup currant jelly and 1 cup water. Bring to a boil, then lower heat. Cook 6 to 8 minutes, until plums are just soft but still retain their shape. Using a slotted spoon, transfer plums to 6 wine glasses.

Raise the heat under the pot to high and cook liquid until reduced to ¾ cup. Spoon reduced liquid over plums. Let cool up to 20 minutes.

Place mascarpone in bowl of an electric mixer and whip until mascarpone looks like thick whipped cream. Dollop mascarpone over plums and, using a small melon baller, scoop out 6 little rounds of currant jelly and place on top to resemble cherries.

Serves 6

Giant Blackberries with Amber Sugar Crystals, Sheep's Milk Yogurt

2 cups thick sheep's milk yogurt, chilled

2 pints very large blackberries (about 48)

⅔ cup sugar

This may be very simple, but the results are incredibly seductive if the yogurt is thick and tangy and the blackberries big and bursting with juice. The crowning glory is a web of caramelized sugar hardened into amber crystals that shatter in your mouth. This is a dessert that has it all: contrasts of sweetness and acidity, sharp edges and smooth curves, and striking colors. If you wait 30 minutes or longer before eating, the bonus is a flavor grace note: an elemental sauce of weeping caramelized and granulated sugars.

Drain yogurt of any excess liquid. Mound in centers of 4 large plates. Equally distribute blackberries among yogurt mounds, sticking approximately 12 blackberries in each.

In a medium nonstick skillet, add all but 1 tablespoon sugar and heat over high heat until sugar begins to melt. Lower heat to medium-high and stir with a wooden spoon until sugar has completely melted into a liquid caramel.

Working quickly, drizzle the caramel over the blackberries and yogurt, being careful not to drip it on the plate (or your fingers—it's very hot!). It will harden quickly.

Sprinkle each mound with a little of the remaining sugar. Serve immediately or wait 30 minutes, as caramel will begin to "weep" and create a sauce around the yogurt.

Serves 4

"Napoleon" of Raspberries and Oranges, Orange Sauce

6 very large oranges

12 ounces fresh raspberries

½ cup sugar

The word napoleon has become part of today's "menu-speak" and only rarely describes a true napoleon, a multilayered pastry separated by layers of pastry cream. My "napoleon" may be multilayered, but here thick slices of sunny oranges stand in for the pastry, with layers of raspberries in between. Use the largest oranges you can find for the most impressive results. More impressive still, my napoleon is fat-free.

Grate rind of 2 oranges to get 1 teaspoon zest. Set aside. Cut the 2 oranges in half and squeeze 1 cup juice. Set aside.

Using a small sharp knife, cut rind from remaining 4 oranges, being sure to remove all the pith. Cut each orange horizontally into perfectly even ¼-inch-thick slices.

On each of 4 large plates place one orange slice. Wash raspberries and dry carefully.

Place 12 berries on each orange slice. Top with a second orange slice and 12 more berries. Top with a third slice of orange and add only 3 berries in center of orange. Refrigerate until cold.

When ready to serve, place sugar, orange juice, and zest in a medium skillet. Bring to a boil. Lower heat and cook until syrupy and reduced to between ½ and ⅔ cup. Let cool a few minutes. Remove napoleons from refrigerator and pour sauce over and around the stack of fruit. Serve immediately.

Serves 4

Blueberries and Roasted Peaches, Fresh Blueberry Syrup

4 cups blueberries

½ cup plus 2 tablespoons sugar

4 very large ripe peaches

Blueberries are now considered the "wonder fruit" because of their abundance of beneficial antioxidants, including anthocyanins, which provide their alluring color (an unusual one for food). I think they're wonderful because of their special flavor and versatility.

TO MAKE BLUEBERRY SYRUP: Wash 2 cups blueberries and dry well, removing any stems. Place blueberries in a small saucepan with ½ cup sugar and 1 cup water. Bring to a boil. Lower heat and cook 20 minutes, until juices thicken. Strain blueberries and liquid through a coarse-mesh sieve, pushing down hard on the blueberries to extract all the juices. You will have approximately 1½ cups syrup. Transfer syrup to a small saucepan.

Wash remaining blueberries and dry well, removing any stems. Set aside.

Preheat oven to 450°F. Cut peaches in half and remove pits. Place, cut side up, on a baking sheet. Sprinkle with 2 tablespoons sugar. Put a little water in the pan. Roast 15 to 20 minutes, until just soft. Place 2 halves on each of 4 dessert plates. Fill with blueberries.

Heat blueberry syrup in saucepan over high heat until it thickens a little. Pour over fruit and serve. Sprinkle with a little more sugar, if desired.

Serves 4

Blueberry *Coeur à la Crème* with Honeyed Blueberries

32 ounces plain low-fat yogurt

⅓ cup plus 3 tablespoons aromatic honey (such as tupelo or lavender)

4 cups fresh blueberries

This unorthodox version of the famous heart-shaped cream cheese dessert is made with yogurt that has been drained to become a thick "cheese." It is as rich and creamy as the classic dessert, but with much less fat.

Drape a 4-cup ceramic *coeur à la crème* mold (with drainage holes) with 2 layers of cheesecloth so that the cheesecloth hangs several inches over the sides of the dish. Or you may line a large sieve with cheesecloth and proceed in the same fashion.

Put the yogurt in a bowl. Stir in ⅓ cup honey and mix thoroughly. Pour into mold and cover with overhanging cheesecloth. Place on a rack in a pan to catch liquid; refrigerate at least 8 hours. Discard liquid.

Several hours before serving, place 3 cups blueberries in a saucepan with remaining 3 tablespoons honey. Bring to a boil. Lower heat and cook 2 minutes. Let compote cool. Refrigerate until cold.

Unmold thickened yogurt, turning onto a large plate. Pour blueberry compute over yogurt. Top with remaining 1 cup blueberries and drizzle with additional honey, if desired.

Serves 4

Cavaillon Melon with Glazed Cherries, Cherry Ice

1½ pounds ripe dark cherries

¼ cup plus ½ cup vanilla sugar

2 large ripe Cavaillon melons

While working on this recipe, Carême came to my mind. This eminent French chef, who worked under Talleyrand, linked the art of cooking to music and painting when he wrote, "Culinary combinations appeal to the sense of sight and color and, through their harmony, they are as seductive as sweet melodies." The visual impact of garnet cherries and orange-fleshed melon sings to me, as it will to you if you use fruit that is perfectly ripe, when its perfume is most intoxicating. Very small sweet cantaloupes can be substituted for the Cavaillon melons, which may not be found so easily. The best ones come from France during late spring and summer.

TO MAKE CHERRY ICE: Remove pits from ¾ pound cherries. Place in bowl of a food processor. Process until very smooth. In a small saucepan bring 1¼ cups water and ¼ cup vanilla sugar to a boil. Boil 2 minutes. Let cool. Add cooled syrup to processed cherries. Process again until smooth. Transfer to a shallow metal dish. Freeze 3 hours, scraping with a fork every 30 minutes to break up ice crystals. Process briefly in food processor just before serving.

Using a small sharp knife, cut melons in half horizontally. You may also create a crown effect by inserting the tip of a small knife around the circumference of the melon in a zigzag fashion. Separate halves carefully. Remove seeds and place seeds in a small bowl lined with 2 layers of paper towels.

Pit cherries carefully, trying to keep them whole. Place in a saucepan with ½ cup vanilla sugar. Let sit 30 minutes. Gently squeeze paper towels with seeds to extract as much melon juice as possible. Add juice and 2 tablespoons water to cherries. Bring to a boil and lower heat to medium-high. Cook 10 minutes, until cherries soften but still retain their shape. Using a slotted spoon, transfer cherries to centers of melon halves. Let cool. Cook juices in saucepan until reduced to a syrupy consistency. Set aside.

Top each melon half with a small scoop of cherry ice. Spoon syrup over top. Serve immediately.

Serves 4

Melon Tartare with Raspberries, Raspberry Coulis

2½ pints fresh raspberries

¼ cup vanilla sugar

1 large ripe cantaloupe or Crenshaw melon

When you see the word "tartare" on a menu it usually means raw and minced, which is the case here. Luscious, sweet blackberries in season can be substituted for the raspberries with great success, and honeydew melon can be substituted for the cantaloupe. At a midsummer night's party, it would be dreamy to serve both.

Wash raspberries. Place 1 pint raspberries in a small saucepan with vanilla sugar and 1⅓ cups water. Bring to a rapid boil. Lower heat and simmer 20 minutes. Strain through a fine-mesh sieve, pressing down firmly on the raspberries to release all the liquid. You will have about 1 cup raspberry coulis. Refrigerate until cold.

Cut melon into 6 wedges and remove seeds. Cut flesh away from rind. Discard rind.

Carefully dice melon into ¼-inch cubes. Pack melon into a 3½-by-1½-inch ring mold* and then remove ring. Or pack into a custard cup and turn out. Repeat process on each of 6 dessert plates.

Place remaining whole raspberries on top of each mound to cover completely. Drizzle with raspberry coulis.

Serves 6

*You can make a ring mold by removing top and bottom from a 6-ounce tuna can.

Cantaloupe with Lemon Verbena

1 large bunch lemon verbena

1 cup sugar

2 very ripe small cantaloupes

Fragrant, sweet cantaloupe and lemon verbena make a compelling team and a very elegant last-minute dessert. Here, large and tiny balls of ripe cantaloupe are bathed in a dulcet herb syrup, then bejeweled with herbed sugar. Herbs in desserts have become quite fashionable lately (although my first encounter with such a marriage was in 1980 at Troisgros in Roanne, France, where I had a memorable apple tart with tarragon). You could use the concept with a variety of melons and herbs: honeydew and peppermint, Cavaillon and lavender, canary melon and basil.

Wash lemon verbena and thoroughly pat dry. Chop enough to get ⅓ packed cup. Set remaining leaves aside for garnish. Place sugar in bowl of a food processor and add chopped lemon verbena. Process until lemon verbena is incorporated. Set ¼ cup of the herb sugar aside for later. Place remaining sugar in a small saucepan with ½ cup water and a pinch of salt. Bring to a boil and cook 2 minutes, until sugar is dissolved. Let cool 10 minutes.

Cut melons in half and scoop out seeds. Scoop out flesh, leaving 2 of the shells intact. Cut these 2 halved shells in half, making 4 "dishes" in which to serve the melon. Using a large and a small melon baller, scoop balls from melon flesh.

If serving immediately, pile melon balls high in melon rind "dishes" and pour warm herb syrup over. Let come to room temperature. Immediately before serving, sprinkle melon with remaining herb sugar and garnish with lemon verbena leaves.

If serving later, place melon balls in a large bowl and pour warm syrup over. Cover and refrigerate until ready to serve. Let come to room temperature. Serve in wine glasses or dessert coupes. Sprinkle with herb sugar and garnish with lemon verbena leaves.

Serves 4

Watermelon Balls
in Watermelon Lemonade

5 pounds ripe red and/or yellow watermelon

4 large lemons

½ cup sugar

I invented watermelon lemonade for my personal trainer, "Thor," so we could have something scrumptious and refreshing after our workout. Then I turned the drink into the perfect hot-weather dessert—equally refreshing, and very appealing when served in a frosted pilsener glass. This also is a lovely midafternoon summer snack, served with a plate of 1-2-3 cookies (pages 108-116).

Remove seeds from watermelon, saving a few for garnish. Using a medium-size melon baller, scoop enough melon balls to get 4 cups. Cover and refrigerate until cold.

Cut flesh from remaining watermelon, including any flesh left from making the melon balls, into 1-inch pieces. Cut 3 lemons in half and squeeze to get ½ cup juice.

Working in 2 batches, blend chopped watermelon and lemon juice in a food processor or blender until very smooth. Transfer to a pitcher.

Bring 1¾ cups water and the sugar to a boil in a medium saucepan over high heat, stirring until sugar dissolves. Add hot syrup to pitcher with watermelon mixture. Refrigerate watermelon lemonade until very cold, about 2 hours. (Adjust flavor with more lemon juice or sugar.)

Put ⅔ cup melon balls into 6 tall glasses—pilsener glasses are ideal. Pour watermelon lemonade over watermelon balls. Garnish with thin slices of remaining lemon.

Serves 6

Purple Figs with Ricotta Cake, Honey-Fig Coulis

2 15-ounce containers ricotta

1½ pounds small ripe purple figs (about 18)

⅓ cup aromatic honey (buckwheat, leatherwood, or wild thyme)

This dessert, trés elegante, tastes like a summer vacation overlooking the Mediterranean. Since fresh ricotta is difficult to find, I use commercial ricotta, but drain some of its liquid. As it sits overnight in cheesecloth-lined custard cups, the cheese sets up into condensed "cakes" ready for a crowning touch of ripe honeyed figs.

Place ricotta in a fine-mesh sieve set over a bowl to catch any liquid. Let sit 45 minutes. Cut six 6-inch squares of cheesecloth and place in each of 6 custard cups. Equally distribute drained cheese into the cups and fold overhanging cheesecloth over top. Place 3 custard cups on top of one another to weight down. Place a custard cup on top of each stack with a little water in it for weight. Refrigerate overnight.

When ready to serve, make the honey-fig coulis: Wash 6 of the smaller figs. Remove stems and cut figs into large chunks. Place in a blender with 2 tablespoons honey and 6 tablespoons water. Blend on high speed several minutes until very smooth and thick. You will have ¾ cup coulis. Set aside.

Unmold custard cups onto 6 large dessert plates. Wash remaining figs and remove stems. Cut lengthwise into 4 wedges each. Place wedges on top of each ricotta cake and drizzle with remaining honey.

Serves 6

Fresh Figs in Nightgowns

12 large ripe purple figs

1 cup Nutella

1½ cups plain yogurt

On one of the hottest days of the year, in my air-conditionless pantry, my Nutella (chocolate-hazelnut spread) had become the consistency of molten chocolate. As it is quite sweet, I mixed it with yogurt, and one by one dipped a whole basket of fleshy purple figs into the mixture. I placed them in the refrigerator, whereupon the coating firmed up to make a very seductive dessert. My husband named them.

Wash figs and pat dry. Set aside.

Put Nutella in a warm place so that it is easy to spoon. Or place the jar in a bowl of very hot water. Spoon Nutella into a clean, dry bowl. Whisk in 1 cup yogurt until completely smooth.

One by one, dip each fig into the mixture, holding it by its stem. Cover each fig completely or almost completely with a thin coating. Place on a large plate lined with waxed paper. Refrigerate until very cold.

Serve with a few tablespoons of plain yogurt alongside. This looks great presented on fresh fig, grape, or lemon leaves. Serve immediately with a fork and a knife.

Serves 4

Note: If you don't feel like dipping the figs, you can serve them whole with a ramekin of the sauce on the side, or cut the figs in half lengthwise and generously drizzle with the sauce.

Pamplemousse Parisien

5 large grapefruit

⅓ cup plus ¼ cup vanilla sugar

3 tablespoons framboise*

Paris in the Fifties by award-winning journalist Stanley Karnow (Random House, 1997) is an evocative chronicle of postwar Paris, when desserts such as this were de rigueur. It is a simple, refreshing grapefruit dessert that cleanses the palate after a rich meal. Read the book after dessert.

Remove the rinds of 2 grapefruits with a vegetable peeler and set rinds aside.

Working over a bowl to catch the juices, use a small sharp knife to cut the skins and white pith off each of the grapefruit, exposing the flesh. Cut between the membranes to release the individual segments. Chill until needed.

Place the juice from the grapefruit in a small saucepan with ⅓ cup vanilla sugar, 1 cup water, and the framboise. Bring to a boil; simmer 15 minutes, or until reduced to ¾ cup. Pour the syrup through a fine-mesh sieve. Let cool and then chill until ready to use.

To make the crystallized grapefruit: Remove pith from the reserved rinds, then cut rind into strips ⅛ inch wide by 2 inches long. Place in a small saucepan with water to cover. Boil 20 minutes then drain. Repeat the process two more times, discarding the cooking water each time. After cooking, put the rind and ¼ cup vanilla sugar in the saucepan. Simmer a few minutes, until the sugar is incorporated and the rinds are clear. Let cool.

Place the grapefruit segments, overlapping, on 6 dessert plates. Pour 2 tablespoons of the framboise syrup over each. Garnish with a mound of crystallized grapefruit and optional sorbet.

TO MAKE GRAPEFRUIT-FRAMBOISE SORBET: Put 1½ cups water in a small saucepan. Add ¾ cup vanilla sugar and bring to a boil. Lower heat and simmer several minutes until liquid is clear. Let cool. Add 1½ cups freshly squeezed grapefruit juice and 3 tablespoons framboise. Chill untill very cold, then freeze in an ice cream maker according to manufacturer's directions.

Serves 6

*Framboise is a raspberry liqueur available in most liquor stores.

Broiled Ruby Grapefruit with Mint Syrup

1 large bunch spearmint

1 cup sugar

2 large ruby grapefruit

Donna Hay is an Australian food writer whose work exemplifies a new style of cooking based on high-quality pristine ingredients and their unadulterated flavours (as she spells it). This mint-glazed grapefruit makes me feel like a kindred spirit, and hers was the inspiration for my dish.

Place sugar in bowl of a food processor. Wash mint and dry thoroughly. Chop enough mint to get ⅔ cup and add to sugar. Process until mint is incorporated. Set half of the minted sugar aside for later. Place the other half in a small saucepan with ¼ cup water. Bring to a boil and cook 1 to 2 minutes, until sugar is dissolved. Let cool and set syrup aside.

Preheat broiler. Halve the grapefruits. Using a small knife, cut around circumference and between membranes to loosen segments. Dry grapefruit tops with paper towels. Sprinkle grapefruits heavily with remaining minted sugar and place on a baking sheet. Broil several minutes, until sugar has caramelized.

Garnish with sprigs of remaining mint and serve with a small pitcher of mint syrup.

Serves 4

Grapefruit "Martini"

4 very large white grapefruit

¾ cup best-quality orange marmalade

4-inch piece fresh ginger

So stimulating, this dessert would make a great prelude to a meal. The flavors of this simple trilogy seem to sparkle on your tongue. Place your martini glasses in the freezer for 30 minutes for a frosty look. Then serve, straight-up, with a grapefruit twist.

Using a small sharp knife, cut all the rind from 1 grapefruit in long thin strips, making sure to also remove the white pith from the rind and from the flesh. Set strips of rind aside. Cut the rind and pith from all the grapefruits. Holding grapefruit over a bowl to catch juices, cut between membranes to release segments and place segments in a large bowl.

Collect 1 cup of the juices and place in a small saucepan with marmalade. Bring to a boil, stirring until smooth, and pour over the grapefruit segments.

Peel ginger with a sharp knife. Grate on the large holes of a box grater and place the shaved ginger in 2 layers of paper towels. Squeeze the ginger over a small bowl to extract 1½ to 2 tablespoons juice. Add to bowl with grapefruit. Cover and chill several hours, until very cold.

Chill 4 large martini glasses. Fill with grapefruit and top with juices to cover. Garnish with a long, thin strip of grapefruit rind. Serve immediately.

Serves 4

Oranges à la Greque

6 large navel oranges

1¾ cups sugar

⅓ cup grenadine

I had the pleasure of knowing Nika Hazelton, who, late in her life, was awarded the title Grande Dame by the prestigious organization Les Dames d'Escoffier. Nika, who lived all over Europe, was one of the original "foodies" (although I'm certain she'd hate that word) and authored dozens of highly respected cookbooks. This is an adaptation of her Greek Oranges from France, served often at her home; she noted that "they were pretty to look at and so perfectly delicious that they were more than worth the trouble."

Using a small, sharp knife, cut the skin (without the pith) from 5 of the oranges. Cut it into tiny strips with a pair of kitchen scissors or a sharp knife. Plunge the strips into a pot of boiling water and boil 2 minutes. Drain and repeat the process two more times, changing the water each time. Set aside.

Cut away the white pith from all the oranges, using a very sharp knife and holding oranges over a bowl in order to save the juice. Cut the oranges in half through the equator and remove any seeds. Place the halved oranges in a large glass bowl, rounded sides up.

Put sugar and 4 cups water in a saucepan and boil 10 minutes. Add grenadine and stir. Pour the hot syrup over the oranges and let stand 15 minutes. Drain syrup back into saucepan and boil again 20 to 25 minutes, until reduced to 2 cups. Put blanched peel on oranges and pour hot syrup over them. Let cool. Cover and refrigerate at least 8 hours.

Serves 6

Sweet Apple Frittata

6 large Golden Delicious apples

1 cup confectioners' sugar

7 extra-large eggs

Follow my instructions and you'll learn the technique for glacéed apples: the fruit will be pale and almost crystallized. At this point the apples become addictive and can be eaten by themselves or topped with crème fraîche and a dusting of confectioners' sugar. Follow the recipe to its completion and you'll be rewarded with a voluptuous egg pancake studded with translucent apples. Try it with a trou normand, which is simply a shot of Calvados.

Preheat the oven to 300°F. Peel and core the apples. Cut each into 8 wedges. Spray a baking dish with nonstick vegetable cooking spray. Arrange apples in a single layer. Sprinkle with all but 3 tablespoons sugar. Add ¼ cup water.

Bake apples 15 minutes. Increase heat to 400°F. Bake 15 minutes. Increase heat to 500°F. and bake 15 minutes longer. Stir twice during baking. Total cooking time is 45 minutes. Spray a 9- or 9½-inch metal pie pan with cooking spray and, using a slotted spoon, transfer apples to pan. Spread evenly in pan to make one thick layer. Let cool.

Pour pan juices into a small saucepan and cook over high heat until juices are reduced to a syrupy consistency, about 3 tablespoons. Set aside.

Beat eggs with an electric mixer until thick, about 5 minutes at high speed. Add reduced juices and a pinch of salt. Beat again. Spoon mixture over room temperature apples. Bake 25 minutes, until set.

Remove frittata from oven. Let cool 5 minutes and turn over onto a large flat plate. Serve at room temperature, cut into wedges. Dust with remaining sugar pushed through a sieve.

Serves 6

Cinnamon-Baked Apples with Apple Butter

4 large Cortland apples

8 teaspoons plus ⅓ cup cinnamon-sugar

½ cup apple butter

The aroma of cinnamon-kissed baked apples wafting through your kitchen will trigger feelings of yearning and nostalgia. I suggest using ruddy Cortlands instead of traditional Rome apples because they're less mealy and more flavorful. And by substituting apple butter for the real butter used in most renditions, you get a more healthful—and more unusual—dessert. The veneer of cinnamon sauce contributes another layer of flavor.

Preheat oven to 400°F.

Cut a thin slice from top of apples. Core apples, removing any seeds, leaving the flesh ½ inch thick at the apples' base. Also cut a small slice from bottom of apples so they don't wobble. Sprinkle inside of each apple with 1 teaspoon cinnamon-sugar. Fill each hole with about 2 tablespoons apple butter. Dust top of each evenly with 1 teaspoon cinnamon-sugar.

Placed filled apples in a shallow baking dish or pie pan. Add ½ inch water. Bake 45 to 50 minutes, until tender. Let cool to room temperature.

Put remaining ⅓ cup cinnamon-sugar and ½ cup water in a small saucepan. Bring to a boil and boil 1 minute. Lower heat to a simmer and cook, stirring constantly, until it is the consistency of thick honey. Whisk in 3 tablespoons water and stir until smooth. Remove from heat. Drizzle baked apples with warm or room-temperature sauce, and serve.

Serves 4

Poached Apples with Crème Fraîche and Cider Syrup

4 large Red Delicious, Gala, or other apples

4 cups unpasteurized apple cider

¾ cup crème fraîche

This is the ultimate autumn dessert, best made with a variety of local apples from your favorite farmers' market. This is also the time of year when apple cider is at its best; when boiled down to a syrup, it becomes an exaggeration of itself.

Using a vegetable peeler or a small sharp knife, carefully peel apples. Cut in half vertically. Using a large melon baller, scoop out the core and seeds.

Place apple halves in a large saucepan or small pot. Cover with cider. Bring to a boil. Lower heat to a simmer and cook until apples are just tender but still retain their shape, 15 to 20 minutes.

Remove apples with a slotted spoon. (At this point, you may leave the apples at room temperature or refrigerate until cold.) Place 2 halves in each of 4 flat soup plates.

Bring apple cider back to a boil. Cook over high heat until cider is reduced to ¾ cup, about 30 minutes. Let cool.

Spoon cider syrup over apples and top with crème fraîche. Serve immediately.

Serves 4

Roasted Grapes with Asian Pears and Gorgonzola, Grape Syrup

2 pounds purple seedless grapes

⅔ pound imported Italian Gorgonzola

2 large Asian pears

Here, lusty purple grapes become a roasted fruit to reckon with and a sweet syrup to marvel at. Asian pears, crunchy and sweet, are a great foil for the ultra-creamy cheese. Real Italian Gorgonzola is truly my favorite food, and I go to great lengths to find the best, especially for this dessert.

TO MAKE GRAPE SYRUP: Wash grapes and pat dry. Remove stems. Place 1 pound grapes in a small saucepan with ½ cup water. Bring to a rapid boil. Lower heat to medium and cover pot. Cook 20 minutes, stirring often. Let cool 10 minutes and place grapes and liquid in bowl of a food processor. Process until very smooth. Return to saucepan and bring to a boil, carefully skimming any foam from the surface. Lower heat to a simmer and cook 15 minutes, or until liquid is reduced to ⅔ cup. Strain through a fine-mesh sieve and set aside.

Preheat oven to 400°F. Place remaining grapes on a baking sheet. Roast 20 to 30 minutes, until lightly caramelized, shaking the baking sheet often to prevent grapes from sticking. Remove from oven and let cool.

Cut cheese into 4 slices. Divide among 4 large plates. Let cheese come to room temperature. Peel pears and cut into fine julienne. Place a mound next to cheese and surround cheese with roasted grapes. Drizzle grape syrup around cheese and fruit.

Serves 4

Slow-Baked Pears with Port and Stilton

1½ cups ruby port

4 ripe large Bartlett pears

½ pound Stilton cheese

It's not just the juxtaposition of these compatible foods that makes this dish special, but how two of the ingredients are manipulated to maximize their essence. Pears are roasted, port wine is reduced, and a simple cheese course is magically transformed into dessert.

Place port in a saucepan and bring to a boil. Lower heat to medium and cook until port is reduced to ½ cup, about 20 minutes. Set aside and let cool.

Preheat oven to 350°F. Wash pears and cut in half lengthwise. Remove seeds and cores from pears and place cut side up on a baking sheet. Bake 20 minutes. Turn pears over and bake 20 minutes longer. Turn over and, using a pastry brush, brush pears with a little of the reduced port. Bake 10 minutes longer. Remove from oven and let cool to room temperature.

Cut pear halves in half lengthwise. Place 4 wedges skin side down on each of 4 plates. Slice cheese into thin slices and place on pears. Drizzle reduced port around fruit and cheese, and serve.

Serves 4

Pear and Cranberry Charlottes, Cranberry Syrup

1½ cups sugar

7 large ripe pears

12 ounces fresh whole cranberries

Celebrate autumn's poster fruit by using a mélange of all the pears available in your local farmers' market. The sweet-acid synergy of pears and cranberries makes this fat-free dessert especially welcome after a robust holiday meal. I love it cold, packed into ramekins and flipped out like little charlottes, afloat in a puddle of warm cranberry syrup; and I love it warm, served from a lovely cut-glass bowl. The cranberry syrup is something you will want to keep around all the time to drizzle over pancakes, to spoon over ice cream, to sweeten your tea.

Bring 3 cups water and the sugar to a boil in a medium pot. Peel pears and remove seeds. Cut each into 6 wedges. Add to boiling sugar syrup, then add cranberries and stir gently. Lower heat to medium and cook about 25 minutes, until pears are tender but still retain their shape.

Line six 5- or 6-ounce ramekins or custard cups with plastic wrap. Use a large enough piece so that the plastic wrap hangs over the sides of the ramekins by several inches. Or you can make 1 large charlotte by using a 6-cup soufflé dish. Set ramekins in a large shallow dish to catch any liquid.

With a slotted spoon, remove pears and cranberries from the pot, letting excess liquid drain into pot. Place fruit in ramekins, packing in tightly. Let cool. Fold overhanging plastic over tops of ramekins. Weight each one down with a can or other weight. Refrigerate overnight.

Strain the cranberry-pear liquid remaining in the pot through a fine-mesh sieve into a smaller saucepan. Cook over medium-high heat until syrup is reduced to 1½ cups. Syrup should be the consistency of honey. Cover and set aside at room temperature.

When ready to serve, unmold charlottes. Gently reheat cranberry syrup and pour over fruit.

Serves 6

Note: This dish can also be served warm, right after cooking the fruit. Remove fruit with a slotted spoon to a decorative glass bowl or individual wine glasses. Cook liquid in pot until reduced to 1½ cups and pour over fruit. Serve warm.

Mangoes in Sweet Lime Syrup, Lime Granita

3 large ripe mangoes

1½ cups sugar

8 large limes

Mangoes are my favorite fruit. I love their resiny perfume and worship their succulent, dense flesh. My Hungarian grandparents had a big old mango tree in their West Palm Beach backyard, and I never eat one without thinking of them. Add a splash of vodka for an added thrill. More thrills? Sprinkle with chili powder or sweet Hungarian paprika.

Using a small sharp knife, peel mangoes. Navigating around the pit, cut the mango flesh into long thick slices. Place in a medium pot. Add ½ cup sugar and 1 cup water. Squeeze 3 limes to get ½ cup juice. Add to pot with mangoes. Bring to a boil. Lower heat to medium and cook 10 minutes. Let cool, then cover and refrigerate until very cold.

TO MAKE LIME GRANITA: Grate rind of remaining limes to get 1 tablespoon zest. Set aside. Cut remaining limes in half and squeeze to get 1 cup lime juice. Add to a saucepan with 2 cups water and 1 cup sugar. Bring to a boil and cook 1 minute, until sugar dissolves. Pour into a pie pan. Let cool and add lime zest. Place in freezer for about 3 hours, scraping with a fork every 30 minutes to break up the crystals. (You can also chill the lime mixture and freeze in an ice cream machine to make a sorbet.)

Distribute mangoes and lime sauce among 6 dessert dishes or flat soup plates. Top each serving with a small scoop of granita. Garnish with thin slices of any remaining limes.

Serves 6

Coconut-Glazed Papaya, Papaya-Lime Cream

1 large, long strawberry papaya (about 3½ pounds)

½ cup cream of coconut

5 large limes

There are many varieties of papaya available today, but the sexiest and most perfumed is one known as "strawberry papaya." Graceful and tapered, about 1 foot long, its meaty flesh is bright reddish orange. Cream of coconut is used as a glaze—which not only sweetens the fruit but blackens a bit under the broiler, imparting a curious flavor note. It is also used to make the lime-kissed cream. But if you like the notion of exploiting an ingredient to the max, as I often do, then make a coconut sorbet to top off the whole thing: mix an additional ½ cup cream of coconut with several tablespoons lime juice and ½ cup water and freeze.

Cut papaya lengthwise into 5 wedges. Remove seeds from each piece and discard. Remove flesh from one of the wedges and cut into large chunks. Place in the bowl of a food processor with ¼ cup cream of coconut.

Grate the rind of 2 limes to get 2 teaspoons zest and add to food processor. Cut 3 limes in half and squeeze to get 6 tablespoons juice. Add to processor with a pinch of salt and process several minutes, until very smooth. Place in the refrigerator until ready to use.

Preheat broiler. Pour 1 tablespoon cream of coconut over each wedge to coat completely. Add a few drops lime juice. Slash each wedge across the width into sections about 1½ inches apart. Place on a broiler pan and broil until papaya is glazed and blackened in some spots.

Let cool a little. Serve with chilled papaya cream and wedges or slices of remaining limes. (If you wish, top with a scoop of sorbet.)

Serves 4

Poached Pineapple in Lemon Syrup, Pineapple Granita

1 large ripe sweet pineapple

1 cup sugar

4 large lemons

The flavors of pineapple and lemon reverberate in this bracing dessert, each fruit exaggerating the taste of the other. Prepare the granita as described, or churn the mixture in an ice cream machine to make a pineapple blizzard. You can gild this dessert with crisp pineapple chips, for which you will need an additional small ripe pineapple and ¼ cup sugar. Follow the directions at the end of the recipe.

Using a small sharp knife, remove rind from pineapple. Save fronds for garnish. Cut a ½-inch-thick round from each end and cut into small pieces. Set aside. Cut remaining pineapple into 4 wedges, cutting lengthwise, and discarding woody core.

Place pineapple wedges in a medium pot. Sprinkle ½ cup sugar over pineapple. Grate rind of 2 lemons and add to pot. Cut lemons in half and squeeze to get ⅓ cup juice. Add to pot. Add cold water just to cover, and bring to a boil. Lower heat to medium and cook, covered, 25 minutes, turning once during cooking. Remove pineapple with a slotted spoon and place in a bowl. Over high heat, reduce syrup to 1½ cups. Pour syrup over pineapple. Refrigerate until very cold.

TO MAKE GRANITA: Place reserved small pieces of pineapple in a food processor. Grate rind of remaining lemons, then cut lemons in half and squeeze to get ⅓ cup juice. Add ½ cup sugar and ¾ cup water and process until very smooth. Pour mixture into a 9-by-13-inch metal or glass dish and freeze for 3 hours, scraping with a fork every 30 minutes to break up ice crystals. Or chill the mixture and freeze in an ice cream machine according to the manufacturer's directions.

Serve a wedge of pineapple with syrup. Top with a large scoop of granita or sorbet. Garnish with a few green fronds, or pineapple chips.

TO MAKE PINEAPPLE CHIPS: Preheat oven to 225°F. Line a sheet pan with parchment or use a Silpat sheet and sprinkle with ¼ cup sugar. Peel and core 1 small pineapple and slice into paper-thin slices using a very sharp, thin-bladed knife. Arrange pineapple slices on the sheet pan and place in the oven overnight, or until crisp. Remove from oven.

Serves 4

Maple-Glazed Pineapple
with Toasted Sesame Seeds

1 ripe medium-large pineapple

**1½ to 2 cups
pure maple syrup**

¼ cup sesame seeds

Like so many of these 1-2-3 desserts, the quality of these individual components really matters. So use one of those fabulous new "gold" pineapples, which have an intoxicating perfume, and simmer thick slices in a warm bath of real maple syrup. Unexpected and compelling toasted sesame seeds add a fragrant nutty flavor and a little crunch. You'll have some leftover maple syrup when you serve this dessert, but you can save it and use it on your breakfast pancakes. It will have a lovely pineapple flavor. Be sure to store it in the refrigerator.

Using a small sharp knife, remove all the rind from the pineapple. Save some of the smaller green fronds for garnish.

Cut pineapple horizontally into 4 thick slices. Using a small round cookie cutter or a small sharp knife, cut out the core.

Place pineapple slices in a skillet (preferably one with a cover) large enough to hold them in one layer. Cover with maple syrup, adding more if necessary. Bring to a boil and cover. If you don't have a cover, use a large heatproof plate, or aluminum foil. Lower heat to medium and cook 10 minutes. Remove cover and turn pineapple over. Cook 10 minutes longer. Let cool in syrup.

Place sesame seeds in a small nonstick skillet. Toast seeds over medium heat until golden brown, stirring often. Let cool.

Divide room-temperature or slightly warm pineapple among of 4 shallow soup plates. Cover with 3 tablespoons maple syrup cooking liquid and scatter with 1 tablespoon toasted sesame seeds. Garnish with small pineapple fronds.

Serves 4

Pineapple Carpaccio with Roasted Grapes, Cinnamon Jus

¾ pound small red or green seedless grapes

1 large very ripe pineapple

6 tablespoons cinnamon-sugar

This recipe turned out even more interesting than I imagined: tropical notes of slightly acidic pineapple play against syncopated bursts of sweet grape and warm cinnamon flavors. Slicing pineapple into paper-thin sheets, carpaccio-style, lets you experience the fruit in a pleasing new way.

Preheat oven to 300°F. Wash grapes, remove any stems, and dry well. Place grapes in a metal pie pan or on a shallow baking dish and bake 1 hour, shaking the pan often so they don't stick. Grapes will release much of their juice and shrivel slightly. (If the grapes are large, they may need up to another 30 minutes in the oven.) Let cool.

Using a sharp knife, remove all the rind from the pineapple. Make sure to remove all the "eyes" and any brown spots. Cut pineapple lengthwise into paper-thin slices. Arrange pineapple slices on 6 large dinner plates. Trim the edges of the pineapple to fit neatly within the border of the plate.

In a small bowl, collect 6 tablespoons of the pineapple's juices. Add cinnamon-sugar and let sit 15 minutes, until sugar dissolves. Drizzle cinnamon-sugar jus over pineapple. (Try sprinkling a tiny bit of salt on top for an interesting taste sensation.)

Place roasted grapes evenly on top of pineapple, several inches apart. Let sit for up to 30 minutes before serving to allow juices to mingle.

Serves 6

1-2-3 Apple Ideas

Fill the cavities of large red apples with a mixture of crumbled gingersnaps and honey, or ground toasted walnuts and cinnamon-sugar. Bake 40 minutes at 350°F.

Cook thick peeled rings of a variety of apples in melted apple jelly until just tender. Serve warm with a dollop of chilled crème fraîche.

Try a new-fangled applesauce by adding fresh strawberries or cranberries to apples while cooking. Sweeten with aromatic honey like wild thyme or leatherwood.

Make an apple fool. Cook apples with cinnamon-sugar until soft and the consistency of applesauce. Let cool and fold into vanilla yogurt or whipped cream. Sprinkle with more cinnamon-sugar.

1-2-3 Berry Ideas

Sprinkle halved strawberries with sugar. Let sit 30 minutes. Cover with Beaujolais.

Freeze super-ripe strawberries. Blend in a blender with coconut milk and vanilla sugar for a great smoothie.

Place washed and halved berries in a shallow casserole. Whip heavy cream until thick. Spread over berries and dust heavily with dark brown sugar. Place under broiler until bubbly.

Make a quick strawberry soup. Sprinkle large berries with confectioners' sugar and roast for 10 minutes at 500°F. Puree with more sugar and buttermilk. Chill until very cold. Top with finely diced berries.

Fill small store-bought meringue shells with purchased English lemon curd. Top with very ripe black raspberries. Crush an additional meringue and scatter on top.

Mix thick, Greek-style yogurt with ginger marmalade. Fold in plump blackberries or blueberries.

Whip crème fraîche with a few tablespoons of crème de cassis or framboise. Layer raspberries and crème fraîche in tall champagne flutes.

Puree ½ pound very ripe berries with 2 tablespoons sugar. Stir into sweetened whipped cream or vanilla yogurt. Add a handful of whole berries. Drizzle with caramelized sugar.

1-2-3 Cherry Ideas

Make a chilled cherry soup with star anise: Combine 1½ pounds pitted fresh cherries, 2½ cups water, ½ cup sugar, and 6 whole star anise. Cook over high heat for 20 minutes. Remove fruit and reduce juices by half. Mix together and chill until cold.

Try Turkish Cherry Bread: Toast thick slices of brioche. Combine 1¼ pounds pitted cherries and ¾ cup sugar in a saucepan. Let sit 30 minutes then cook with ⅓ cup water until soft and a syrup forms. Pour hot cherries and syrup over toast.

Cook pitted red cherries in tawny port until tender. Chill. Serve with Devonshire or clotted cream.

1-2-3 Citrus Fruit Ideas

Place sections of grapefruit in flat soup plates. Reduce guava nectar until it is thick and syrupy. Chill and pour over grapefruit. Garnish with julienned mint.

Toss grapefruit and orange segments together with cassis and juices from the 2 fruits. Serve in chilled wine glasses with a scoop of cassis granita made with equal parts of crème de cassis and water and some grated zest.

Make Colman Andrews' polenta dessert: Prepare quick-cooking polenta and top with lots of thin slices of blood oranges, without the rind. Sprinkle with sugar.

Three simple orange salads. Remove rind from juice oranges and slice into ¼-inch thick rounds. 1) Sprinkle heavily with confectioners' sugar and cinnamon; 2) Splash with dark rum and top with lots of toasted coconut; or 3) toss with pomegranate seeds and drizzle with honey.

1-2-3 Fig Ideas

Cut ripe purple figs in half through the stem end. Slice paper-thin slices of halvah and scatter on top. Drizzle with aromatic honey.

Split figs into quarters, going only half-way to the bottom. Spread wedges slightly. Fill centers with whipped cream. Pour melted Toblerone over cream and figs.

Cut a round from panettone that is 1 inch thick and 4 inches in diameter. Toast lightly. Pile high with ripe, sliced or quartered figs. Spoon warm buckwheat honey on top. Sprinkle with toasted crumbs made from additional panettone.

Cut a cross halfway down the stem end of fresh figs. Whip fresh goat cheese with lemon or bitter orange marmalade. Stuff each fig with this mixture. Melt some of the marmalade with a little water. Using a pastry brush, glaze each fig.

1-2-3 Fruit and Cheese Ideas

Sweet red cherries and toasted hazelnuts, ripe Camembert

Fresh figs with a drizzle of wild thyme honey, Italian Gorgonzola

Forelle pears and Medjool dates, runny Taleggio

A variety of sliced plums and mint, fresh sheep's milk cheese

Dried pears and champagne grapes, Roquefort

Big, plump blackberries with lemon curd, fresh goat cheese

Ripe peaches and fresh fennel, creamy blue

Prunes splashed with Armagnac, St. André or Brillat-Savarin

Roasted grapes and whole almonds, Cabrales

Dried figs with fennel seeds, St. Marcellin

Thin slices of watermelon with and honey, creamy feta

Bosc pears, peeled and sliced, splashed with Midori, Parmigiano-Reggiano shards

Local apples, peeled and drizzled with cider syrup, Pont l'Eveque

Toasted walnut or date-nut bread and roasted peaches, mascarpone

Concord or local purple grapes and lemon marmalade, drained ricotta cheese

Sweet honeydew and sun-dried cherries, brie

1-2-3 Melon Ideas

Using a melon baller, scoop out ½-inch balls from very ripe cantaloupe or cassava melon. Marinate in sweet vermouth. Sprinkle with crushed amaretti cookies.

Make a flavor-packed melon granita Use ½ pound of any ripe melon and puree with ⅓ cup white port and ¼ cup sugar. Pour into shallow pan and freeze, stirring every 30 minutes until frozen. Serve with tiny melon balls.

You'll love tequila melon. Make balls from a ripe deep-orange melon, such as Charentais or cantaloupe. Toss with good tequila and sugar, about ½ cup tequila to ¼ cup sugar. Add salt and freshly ground black pepper to taste.

Melon from Provence: Cut Cavaillon melons in half and scoop out the seeds. Fill with a mixture of crème de cassis and water to which gelatin has been added. Chill until the center is firm yet jiggly. Cut into wedges.

1-2-3 Pear Ideas

Poach peeled whole pears in simple syrup mixed with several tablespoons of pickling spice. Cook until just tender. Cool in liquid and refrigerate until very cold.

Peel ripe pears and cut into thin wedges. Place in wine goblets. Melt bittersweet chocolate with a little vanilla ice cream until smooth and hot. Pour over pears. Top with a scoop of ice cream.

Cook peeled pears in sweet Marsala and water until tender. Remove fruit and reduce juices until syrupy. Roll pears in crushed amaretti cookies. Serve with reduced Marsala.

Poach peeled pear halves in simple syrup made with vanilla-sugar. Make almond brittle by melting vanilla-sugar until it is liquid caramel and stirring in sliced toasted almonds. Let harden. Crack into small pieces and scatter on top of pears.

1-2-3 Rhubarb Ideas

Poach sliced rhubarb and wedges of mango in simple syrup. Puree half of the fruit and liquid until very smooth. Freeze and scrape up every 30 minutes until frozen. Serve fruit with a scoop of granita.

Make a chilled rhubarb soup. Cook diced rhubarb with vanilla-sugar until very soft. Top with heavy cream or mascarpone, whipped with a little sugar.

1-2-3 Stone Fruit Ideas

Cut ripe peaches in half. Replace pit with a nugget of marzipan. Sprinkle with orange-flower water and bake at 450°F. for 5 minutes.

Slice ripe nectarines into thin wedges. Place in martini glasses. Pour equal amounts of Campari and simple syrup over fruit.

Cut nectarines in half and roast for 20 minutes at 450°F., turning once or twice. Let cool. Fill cavities with lightly whipped cream. Reduce Amaretto until thick and syrupy and pour over fruit and cream.

Make Apricots in Cinnamon Syrup. Cut 2 pounds apricots in half. Add 2 cups water, ⅛ cup dark brown sugar, 4 cinnamon sticks, and 1 teaspoon black peppercorns. Cook until tender. Remove fruit and reduce juices until syrupy. Combine with fruit and chill.

Cut ripe Italian plums in half. Fill each with lemon yogurt that has been drained until thick. Sprinkle with coarsely chopped pistachio nuts.

Cut ripe peaches into quarters. Saute in sweet butter until golden. Add Southern Comfort and cook over high heat until fruit begins to caramelize. Serve warm.

1-2-3 Tropical Fruit Ideas

Halve ripe papayas and scoop out seeds. Fill with raspberries and top with lime sorbet.

Cut thin slices of ripe mango. Top with a sorbet made from cream of coconut and fresh lime juice. Sprinkle with grated lime zest.

Freeze a can of lychees in syrup. Make a fruit salad of diced mango and kiwi. Puree lychees in food processor until a smooth sorbet is formed. Serve on fruit.

Cut pineapple into very thin slices. Melt vanilla-sugar until caramelized. Pour over fruit. It will harden. Top with julienned mint or crushed pistachios.

Peel kiwi and cut into thin wedges. Place in wine glasses. Make a syrup of honey and fresh lemon juice and pour over kiwi.

Going bananas: 1) Slice bananas thinly and ladle Chocolate Yogurt (page 124) on top; 2) Cut bananas into large chunks and toss with clementine segments and Grand Marnier; or 3) Cut in half lengthwise and then crosswise to make 4 pieces. Sprinkle with cinnamon-sugar, broil, then top with rum raisin ice cream.

Custards and Soufflés

"CUSTARDS ARE THE ESSENCE OF SIMPLICITY," THE LATE JAMES BEARD ONCE SAID.
Over lunch one day, we discussed the emergence of spoonable desserts in trendy restaurants. Was the lack of proper cakes and pastries on menus the result of a declining talent pool of pastry chefs, or was it that crème brûlée had captured everyone's desire for grown-up comfort food? We never agreed on an answer, but dug enthusiastically into our white chocolate pots de crèmes. (You can find this recipe on page 121.)

Whether it's a swirl of fresh lime mousse, a timbale of panna cotta with caramel sauce, strawberry bavarois under a shimmer of ruby aspic, a warm raspberry soufflé, or a bracing lemon pudding under peaks of meringue, what these all have in common is their effable smoothness that begins at the tip of your tongue, floats to the roof of your mouth, then drifts to the back of your throat, where it slowly melts away.

What separates these elegant offerings is, naturally, their taste, but also their temperatures. Coconut rum custard spans two zones: a chilled custard topped with a scoop of frozen coconut sorbet. Sweet baked cheese soufflé is served cold and condenses like a cheesecake as it chills; raspberry soufflé, on the other hand, swells with pride as hot air dramatically puffs it into a cloud of pink.

My three-ingredient alchemy is best expressed in making these custards and soufflés, where pineapple juice, sugar, and eggs coalesce into a caramel-coated, quivering flan of tropical intensity; where eggs, sugar, and jam magically levitate into a sophisticated (and low-fat) soufflé; where a can of eggnog becomes a holiday flan studded with sun-dried cherries.

Since the ultimate appeal of these desserts is their fragility, it is important to follow the directions carefully. Custards prepared in a double boiler should become very thick and creamy before removing from atop the simmering water; gelatin needs to be dissolved and stirred for several minutes in order to be thoroughly suspended in liquid; egg whites should be whipped until stiff and glossy to retain their shape for mousses, chiffons, and meringues.

Fresh Lime Mousse

5 large limes

½ cup plus 3 tablespoons sugar

6 extra-large eggs

Most desserts lull your senses, but this sassy mousse, with its bracing acidity, actually revs up your tastebuds. I love serving this after a heavy dinner because it gets my guests talking again.

Grate the rind of enough limes to get 1 tablespoon zest. Cut limes in half and squeeze to get ½ cup juice.

Separate egg yolks from egg whites, saving 2 egg whites. (Reserve remaining whites for another use.) Place yolks in a medium metal bowl and stir in ½ cup sugar. Place over a pot of boiling water to create a "double boiler," making sure the bottom of the bowl does not touch the water. Using a wire whisk, whisk vigorously while cooking eggs and sugar for 1 minute. Slowly add lime juice and 2 teaspoons zest and continue to cook 6 to 8 minutes, whisking constantly, until the mixture is the texture of thick pudding. Remove from heat and let cool 5 minutes, whisking frequently.

Place 2 egg whites in bowl of an electric mixer with 3 tablespoons sugar and a pinch of salt. Beat until very stiff and glossy. Fold beaten whites into lime mixture. Stir gently until smooth.

Spoon mousse into 4 wine glasses. Child until very cold. Sprinkle with remaining lime zest. Best served the day it is made.

Serves 4

Crème Caramel

¾ cup plus ½ cup sugar

3 cups half-and-half

4 extra-large eggs plus 2 egg yolks

You can make this most classic of bistro favorites with vanilla sugar, but I love the stark simplicity of regular sugar that you caramelize to a dark amber; it assumes a smoky, honeyed flavor, obliterating any need for vanilla. Also known as crème renversée, it is an infinitely soothing dessert that knows no season.

Preheat oven to 350°F.

In a small nonstick skillet, put ¾ cup sugar. Place over medium-high heat and cook, stirring constantly with a wooden spoon. After 2 to 3 minutes, the sugar will become a dark brown liquid. Immediately pour into six 5-ounce glass custard cups.

Place half-and-half in a medium saucepan and cook over medium-high heat just until bubbles start to form. Remove from heat and let cool 5 minutes. Beat eggs, yolks, and ½ cup sugar in an electric mixer. Slowly add warm half-and-half and a pinch of salt. Mix thoroughly.

Pour mixture into custard cups over the sugar (which by now will have hardened). Place cups in a deep baking pan.

Pour boiling water into pan until it reaches halfway up sides of cups. Bake 40 minutes, or until custard is set. Remove cups from water bath and let cool. Cover and refrigerate until very cold.

Run knife around edges of cups or briefly dip bottoms into hot water. Turn upside down on plates. Custard will come out easily and caramel will form a sauce around the custard.

Serves 6

Warm Raspberry Soufflé

1½ cups best-quality raspberry jam, with seeds

6 extra-large egg whites

½ cup sugar or vanilla sugar

This pink cloud of fluff is a snap to make and is virtually fat-free. Make sure the foil collar reaches way above the top of your dish, since the soufflé swells exponentially as it bakes. It also deflates quickly, so make sure your guests are sitting at the table ready to admire your latest achievement as soon as it comes out of the oven. Celebrate with a glass of demi-sec champagne. Substitute a more exotic jam, like cloudberry or blood orange marmalade, if you wish.

Preheat oven to 400°F.

In a medium saucepan over medium heat, melt the jam with 2 tablespoons water, stirring until smooth. Keep warm.

In the bowl of an electric mixer, beat the egg whites together with all but 1 tablespoon sugar and a pinch of salt until glossy. Using a rubber spatula, fold one-fourth of the mixture into warm jam. Then add jam mixture to the remaining whites, folding gently.

PREPARE A 6-CUP SOUFFLÉ DISH: Make an aluminum-foil collar to rise 3 inches above the rim of the dish by folding a 2-foot length of aluminum foil in half lengthwise; wrap the dish with the foil, then tie in place with string. Coat inside of dish and foil with vegetable cooking spray. Spoon in egg white mixture and sprinkle with remaining 1 tablespoon sugar. Bake 15 to 18 minutes, until puffy and golden; do not open oven door during baking. Remove foil and serve immediately.

Serves 6

Pineapple Flan

1 cup sugar

8 extra-large eggs

2 cups unsweetened pineapple juice

This is a dessert held together by the commitment of just a few ingredients with no goal other than to soothe and beguile. It is a defiant amalgam of highly acidic pineapple juice, sugar, and eggs that results in a wobbly block of tropical tastes. Also delicious made with mango or guava nectar.

Preheat oven to 350°F.

In a small nonstick skillet put ½ cup sugar. Cook over medium-high heat, stirring constantly with a wooden spoon, until sugar melts completely into a dark liquid caramel, about 3 minutes. Coat the insides of 5 custard cups or small ramekins with vegetable cooking spray. Immediately divide the caramel among the cups or ramekins to coat the bottom of each.

Separate the yolks and whites of 4 eggs. (Reserve whites for another use. Or make tiny meringues from whites and additional sugar to serve with the flan.) In the bowl of an electric mixer place 4 egg yolks, 4 whole eggs, and ½ cup sugar. Beat for 1 minute, until eggs and sugar are well blended.

Slowly add pineapple juice, little by little, and continue to mix until juice is incorporated. Do not let the mixture become too frothy. With a ladle, divide mixture evenly among the custard cups.

Place custard cups in a large, deep pan. Create a water bath by adding boiling water to the pan so that the water level comes two-thirds up the sides of the cups. Carefully place in the oven. Bake 40 to 45 minutes, until just set. Remove cups from water bath. Let cool and refrigerate until very cold, preferably overnight.

When ready to serve, carefully unmold cups onto flat dessert plates, loosening the sides with a small sharp knife if necessary. Caramel will coat the top and sides of the flan. Serve immediately.

Serves 5

Eggnog Flan
with Sun-Dried Cherries

5 cups eggnog*

1 cup sun-dried cherries

**5 extra-large eggs
plus 2 egg yolks**

This simple custard is lovely around the holidays. The surface of the flan is coated with a thin layer of reduced eggnog that blackens in patches for a professional-looking finish when run under the broiler. Sun-dried cherries add great texture, color, and taste. Serve with a small snifter of aged rum.

Preheat oven to 350°F.

Put 4 cups eggnog in a large saucepan and bring just to a boil. Lower heat and simmer 5 minutes.

Place sun-dried cherries in a small bowl and pour 2 cups boiling water over cherries. Let sit 5 minutes. Drain thoroughly and pat dry.

Place eggs and egg yolks in bowl of an electric mixer. Beat until blended, then slowly add warm eggnog. Mix thoroughly. Place half of the cherries in bottom of a shallow heatproof 9-by-11-inch casserole. Slowly pour in egg mixture. Place in a deep pan. Add boiling water to come three-quarters up the sides of the casserole. Bake 15 minutes and drop in remaining cherries. Bake 30 minutes longer, or until flan is just set.

Meanwhile, put remaining 1 cup eggnog in a small saucepan and cook over medium heat until thick and reduced to ¼ cup. Remove flan from water bath and immediately spoon reduced eggnog over flan. Place under the broiler about 1 minute, until the surface blackens in patches.

Let cool. Serve at room temperature. Or refrigerate and then let come to room temperature before serving.

Serves 6

*Borden makes a nonrefrigerated eggnog, or you can use a refrigerated eggnog when available.

Maple Chiffon

3 extra-large eggs

½ cup pure maple syrup

**1 cup heavy cream,
whipped and chilled**

The chiffonlike texture of this ethereal mousse is the result of professional, yet easy, techniques. Real maple syrup is responsible for its elemental flavor.

Separate the egg yolks from the egg whites, placing the yolks in the bowl of an electric mixer. Set whites aside. Beat yolks on high speed for 5 minutes, until thick and pale yellow. Add maple syrup and briefly mix. Transfer mixture to a metal bowl and set over a pot of boiling water, making sure the bottom of the bowl does not touch the water. Cook 5 minutes, or longer, stirring constantly, until mixture becomes very thick. Let cool completely.

Beat egg whites together with ⅛ teaspoon salt until stiff. Fold into the yolk mixture. Carefully fold whipped cream into maple mixture. Spoon into 4 or more parfait, martini, or wine glasses. Chill thoroughly, then serve. (If you wish, you can freeze the mixture, and serve with additional warmed maple syrup.)

Serves 4

Coconut Rum Custard
with Coconut Sorbet

1½ cups cream of coconut

¾ teaspoon rum extract

**4 extra-large eggs
plus 2 egg yolks**

Tasting like an island vacation, this is two desserts in one—an ultra-creamy custard and a vivacious sorbet. I like the contrasts of temperature and texture, especially when the custard is served still warm and wobbly and the sorbet cold and smooth.

TO MAKE SORBET: Mix ½ cup cream of coconut with ½ cup water and ¼ teaspoon rum extract. Freeze in an ice cream maker. Or transfer to a metal pie pan and place in freezer for 3 hours, scraping with a fork every 30 minutes to break up ice crystals, until it is slushy but frozen.

Preheat oven to 375°F.

In bowl of an electric mixer, put remaining 1 cup cream of coconut, 1 cup water, eggs, egg yolks, and a pinch of salt. Mix briefly and add remaining ½ teaspoon rum extract. Beat until all the ingredients are thoroughly blended.

Pour mixture into 5 custard cups or small coffee cups. Place cups in a deep pan. Add boiling water to come three-quarters up the sides of the cups. Bake 20 to 22 minutes, or until the custard is just set.

Carefully remove cups from water bath. Let cool. Serve at room temperature with a small scoop of sorbet on top, or chill the custard for several hours, until very cold, then top with a small scoop of sorbet.

Serves 5

Sweet Baked Cheese Soufflé

**32 ounces pineapple
cottage cheese**

**1 cup plus 3 tablespoons
confectioners' sugar**

7 extra-large eggs

On an extraordinary research trip to Sicily one summer, my husband and I had a provincial ricotta cheese dessert that, upon analysis, we determined had been fairly difficult to make. So I simplified it into a three-ingredient soufflé made in a loaf pan. This version tastes vaguely like the dessert I remember, with a texture more refined than rustic.

Preheat oven to 375°F.

Place cottage cheese in bowl of a food processor. Add 1 cup sugar and process until very smooth. With the motor running, add the eggs, one at a time, until just blended.

Coat a 2-quart glass loaf pan with vegetable cooking spray. Pour in cheese mixture. Bake 60 to 70 minutes, until golden brown and puffed. Remove from oven, let cool slightly, about 10 minutes. Run a small sharp knife around the edges of the soufflé and turn out onto a platter; there will be some liquid in the bottom of the dish, so be careful when turning out. Discard any liquid. Before serving, push remaining 3 tablespoons sugar through a sieve and heavily dust top of soufflé. This can be served slightly warm or at room temperature. Cut into thick slices.

Serves 8

Panna Cotta with Caramel Sauce

1⅔ cups plus ½ cup heavy cream

¼ cup plus 6 tablespoons vanilla sugar

1 teaspoon unflavored gelatin

Like crème brûlée, but less daunting, panna cotta *is an ivory-hued, chilled custard judged by its smooth fragility. Literally "cooked cream," and sometimes called* crema cotta, *this dessert originated in Italy's Piedmont region, where it is served unadorned, in small portions. I like to add a little puddle of warm caramel sauce (made with two of the three ingredients) atop the cool custard for a compelling contrast.*

Place 1⅔ cups heavy cream in a medium saucepan. Add ¼ cup vanilla sugar and bring just to a boil. Lower heat and simmer 3 minutes, or until sugar is completely dissolved.

Place 2 tablespoons cold water in a cup. Sprinkle gelatin over water and let sit 30 seconds. Stir and add to warm cream mixture, beating well with a wire whisk. Cook over low heat 1 minute, whisking constantly. Remove from heat and whisk 1 minute. Let cool 10 minutes, whisking frequently to make sure gelatin is thoroughly incorporated.

Divide mixture evenly among 4 or 5 ramekins or small coffee cups. Let cool to room temperature, then refrigerate until set, about 4 hours. Best served within 24 hours. Serve with a little warm caramel sauce.

TO MAKE CARAMEL SAUCE: Place 2 tablespoons water and 6 tablespoons vanilla sugar in a small saucepan. Cook over medium heat, stirring constantly with a wooden spoon, until sugar dissolves and liquid is clear. Increase heat to high and cook until syrup turns dark amber. Remove from heat. Immediately and carefully add ½ cup heavy cream (the mixture will bubble up), stirring constantly. Cook over low heat a few minutes, stirring constantly, until a thick, creamy caramel sauce forms.

Serves 4 or 5

Strawberry-Buttermilk *Bavarois*

**32 ounces frozen
sliced strawberries in syrup**

2 cups buttermilk

4 teaspoons unflavored gelatin

Bavarian cream, or bavarois, *is a cold dessert made from an egg custard stiffened with gelatin, mixed with cream and a fruit puree, then set in a mold. My version has no egg, but the resulting taste is similar, with fewer calories and fat, and sports an equally creamy texture. Simple and refreshing, it makes an unexpectedly fruity finale to a fine meal. The clear layer of aspic is optional. Follow the simple directions below.*

Thaw strawberries and place in bowl of a food processor with buttermilk. Process until very smooth. Transfer to a medium saucepan and bring just to a boil, stirring constantly.

Sprinkle gelatin over ⅓ cup cold water. Let sit 30 seconds, then stir. Over low heat, add gelatin mixture to warm strawberries and continue to cook 1 minute, until gelatin is completely incorporated, stirring constantly until smooth. Let cool 10 minutes, stirring frequently to make sure gelatin is thoroughly incorporated.

Pour mixture into 6 dessert coupes, coffee cups, or martini or wine glasses. Let cool and refrigerate until gelatin is set, at least 4 hours. Serve very cold.

For added complexity, add a clear layer of strawberry aspic: Thaw an additional package of frozen strawberries in a coarse-mesh sieve set over a bowl. Let defrost completely. (Save strawberries to make "Strawberry leather" or for another use.) Heat 1 cup of the juices in a small saucepan. Sprinkle 1½ teaspoons gelatin over 2 tablespoons cold water and let sit 30 seconds. Add to warm strawberry juice and heat 1 minute over medium heat, until gelatin is dissolved. Let cool completely and pour over chilled bavarois. Chill until set.

TO MAKE OPTIONAL STRAWBERRY LEATHER: Puree ⅓ cup reserved berries with 1 tablespoon syrup until smooth. Line a cookie sheet with parchment or Silpat sheet. Spread puree in a very thin layer. Bake at 300°F for 15 to 20 minutes.

Serves 6

A Grand Crème Brûlée

3 cups heavy cream

8 extra-large egg yolks

⅔ cup plus ¼ cup vanilla sugar

This recipe has stolen the heart of every dessert eater in America since it was popularized by Sirio Maccione at New York's Le Cirque sometime in the 1970s. (Before that time, chocolate mousse was it!) I've decided to make one large crème brûlée for a change, since most of us don't own enough—or any—of those classic little crème brûlée dishes. You can make this in one large soufflé dish and present it on a silver platter.

Preheat oven to 350°F.

Put cream in a heavy saucepan and cook over low heat to just below a boil. Lower heat immediately and simmer 2 minutes.

Put egg yolks and ⅔ cup vanilla sugar in bowl of an electric mixer. Beat on high speed until thick, about 1 minute.

Gradually add hot cream to yolks, beating at low speed until just blended. Ladle custard into a 6-cup soufflé dish. Set in a large, deep baking dish. Add boiling water to pan to come almost to the top of the soufflé dish. Bake 1 hour and 15 minutes, or until set. Carefully remove from water bath and let cool. Cover and refrigerate until very cold.

When ready to serve, preheat broiler. Sprinkle crème brûlée with remaining ¼ cup vanilla sugar. Place under broiler, 4 to 6 inches from the heat (or use one of those little propane torches*), to melt the sugar on top of the custard. Watch carefully, as sugar burns quickly. (If using a torch, light the flame and simply touch the surface of the sugar until it melts and turns dark amber.) Let cool a few minutes until sugar hardens, then serve.

Serves 6

*Available at specialty cookware stores.

Orange Custard Roulade

4 large oranges

5 extra-large eggs

¾ cup sugar

Portugal inspired this "dream of laranja" where desserts are characteristically eggy, sweet and flavored with orange or lemon. It has a special texture—not quite a custard, soufflé or a cake—and a bright orange accent, and it is elegant whether served straight from the oven, at room temperature, or cold. Remember Galliano—that herbaceous yellow liqueur once used to make Harvey Wallbangers? Well, a small snifter of it goes beautifully with this dessert.

Preheat oven to 450°F.

Grate rind of enough oranges to get 3 heaping tablespoons zest. Cut oranges in half and squeeze to get ½ cup juice. Remove rind from remaining oranges and cut oranges into thin slices or segments.

In the bowl of an electric mixer, put eggs, 9 tablespoons sugar, ½ cup orange juice, 2 tablespoons zest, and a pinch of salt. Beat on high for 1 minute.

Coat an 8-by-8 inch glass or pyrex pan thoroughly with nonstick cooking spray. Pour the mixture into the pan and bake for 15 minutes, until the top is puffed and golden brown.

Meanwhile, place a clean linen kitchen towel on a board large enough to accommodate the baked custard. Dampen lightly with water and sprinkle with remaining 3 tablespoons sugar. Remove custard from the oven and cool for 5 minutes. Cut around the edges using a small sharp knife. Place board on top of pan, towel side down, and invert custard onto sugared towel. Remove pan. Lift half of the towel and use it to roll the dessert like a jelly roll, about 1½ times. Press down lightly. Gently lift from sugared towel and place roulade on a large plate.

Sprinkle with remaining tablespoon of zest and garnish with slices or segments of oranges. Serve slightly warm, at room temperature, or cold.

Serves 4

Baked Lemon Custard
with Meringue

4 large lemons

⅔ cup plus 4½ tablespoons sugar

8 extra-large eggs

When making this dessert you will perfect two professional techniques: you'll learn how to make custard and how to make a meringue. Or you can skip the meringue and serve the puckery custard in small glasses, warm, in the style of zabaglione.

Grate the rind of enough lemons to get 1½ tablespoons zest. Cut lemons in half and squeeze to get ⅔ cup juice. Set aside.

Separate egg yolks from egg whites, saving 3 egg whites. (Set aside remaining whites for another use.)

Add yolks to a medium metal bowl and stir in ⅔ cup sugar. Place over a pot of boiling water to create a "double boiler," making sure the bottom of the bowl does not touch the water. Stirring constantly with a wire whisk, cook eggs and sugar 1 minute. Slowly add lemon juice and zest and continue to cook, whisking constantly 6 to 8 minutes, until airy and very thick. (You can serve the custard at this point, slightly warm, in small wine glasses.) Spoon mixture into 4 ramekins, leveling off the top. Let cool and then chill until cold.

Preheat oven to 450°F.

Beat 3 egg whites together with 4 tablespoons sugar, until very stiff and glossy. Pile high onto each ramekin, using a small flexible rubber spatula to smooth. The meringue should completely cover the custard and should sit about 3 inches high. Place ramekins on a baking sheet. Sprinkle each lightly with a little of the remaining sugar. Bake 6 to 7 minutes, until meringue is golden. Remove from oven. Let cool and serve.

Serves 4

Rice Pudding with Two Milks

4 cups milk

¾ cup sweetened condensed milk*

⅛ cup long-grain rice

This is a very sweet, very sensuous version of rice pudding that you should serve in small portions. Rice is slowly cooked on top of the stove in a mixture of fresh and condensed milk until it thickens into a soft cream punctuated with bits of rice. I like to steam some additional milk and spoon it on like a frothy cappuccino, or I serve with a dollop of dolce de leche, made from sweetened condensed milk (see below). This gentle dessert should be served warm or at room temperature, as the rice will harden when chilled. For added drama, you can top with shavings of edible silver or gold leaf, available in most Middle Eastern food stores.

In a large saucepan with a cover, whisk together both milks. Add a pinch of salt. Bring just to a boil, stirring often. Lower heat and cook 5 minutes. Reduce heat to very low and add rice. Simmer, covered, for 1 hour, stirring every 10 minutes.

After 1 hour, the rice should be soft and the mixture thick and creamy. Remove cover and stir, uncovered, 1 to 2 minutes, until thick. Spoon mixture into a shallow serving casserole dish, small wine glasses, or elegant coffee cups. Cover with plastic wrap. Serve warm or at room temperature.

You have several serving options: If your rice pudding is in an oven-proof casserole or soufflé dish, you can place it under the broiler 1 minute to brown lightly. Or if your pudding is at room temperature and in wine glasses or individual dishes, you can steam some additional milk in an espresso machine, and spoon some of the froth on top. Or you can top with a dollop of *dolce de leche.*

TO MAKE *DOLCE DE LECHE*: Preheat oven to 350°F. Place 14 ounces condensed milk in a metal pie tin. Cover tightly with foil and place in larger pan. Fill pan halfway with water. Bake 2 hours. Uncover and transfer to a small bowl. Makes about 1 cup.

Serves 4

*If you have a choice of brands of sweetened condensed milk, I recommend Magnolia.

1-2-3 Custard and Soufflé Ideas

Make an old-fashioned blancmange by mixing almond syrup (orzata), softened gelatin, and cream. Pour into a ring mold and chill. Fill center with three mixed berries.

Try a simple lingonberry mousse. Mix imported jarred lingonberries with cooked farina and soft whipped cream.

Enjoy maple custard. Beat 3 eggs together with ½ cup maple syrup and 2 cups half-and-half. Pour into custard cups and bake in a water bath. Chill and flip out. Serve with hot maple syrup.

Substitute a more exotic jam, like cloudberry or blood-orange marmalade, in the recipe for Warm Raspberry Soufflé (page 67).

Whip up a zabaglione for impromptu guests. In a double boiler, whisk together 8 egg yolks, ½ cup sugar, and a liqueur of your choice—from Marsala to Midori.

Make a "cannoli custard" by mixing together drained ricotta cheese, confectioners' sugar, and rum.

Try rich and simple vanilla *pots de crème.* Whisk 4 egg yolks until thick and pale. Add 1¾ cups hot milk and ⅓ cup vanilla-sugar. Bake in pots de crème cups in a water bath for 30 minutes at 375°F.

Make a holiday bread pudding. Cut 8 ounces panettone into large cubes and toast lightly. Mix 2 cups eggnog and 2 eggs and pour over panettone. Place in a waterbath and bake 40 minutes.

Prepare Sauternes Sabayon (page 25) and fold in whipped cream for a stylish pudding. Or serve the sabayon over cubes of Sauternes aspic (stir dissolved gelatin into warm Sauternes and chill), or over Sauternes-soaked berries or pound cake.

Try James Beard's Apple Snow. Beat 3 egg whites until they form stiff peaks. Slowly add ½ cup sugar and beat until glossy. Fold in 1 cup best-quality applesauce.

Refer to the chocolate chapter for more custards, puddings, and soufflés (page 119).

Cakes, Cookies, and Tarts

THE VERY IDEA OF MAKING A CAKE WITH ONLY THREE INGREDIENTS PROVOKES A LOT OF SKEPTICISM.
Invariably the question is, "And one of them is a cake mix, right?" "No," I always say.

I may not be a "domestic goddess" like my favorite British cook, Nigella Lawson, who wrote a book by that
name about baking and the art of comfort cooking, but when it comes to making ethereal three-ingredient cakes,
dreamy fruit tarts, and all manner of cookies, "sorceress" might be an appropriate name for me. In my kitchen,
nuts, sugar, and eggs are magically transformed into Hazelnut Angel Cake; moist Maple Walnut Loaf is made from
walnuts, pure maple syrup, and eggs; crumbly, sugary Peanut Thins are made from peanut butter, turbinado sugar,
and eggs. Invariably the question is, "What, no flour?" "No," I always say.

The wizardry continues with Meringue Nests with Lime Custard (eggs, sugar, limes); Apple Pizza with Cider
Sorbet (puff pastry, apples, real apple cider); Cinnamon Shortbread (self-rising flour, cinnamon-sugar, butter); and
Gianduia Sandwich Cookies (Nutella, flour, eggs).

Most of these desserts are baked, but several rely on the assembly of ingredients to become little cakes in
themselves. For example, Strawberry Summer Cake is made from ladyfingers, sugar, and super-ripe strawberries.

Many of the baked goods use frozen puff pastry dough that is then rolled, stretched, or cut according to the recipes'
requirements. Depending on where you live, you can sometimes get great-quality puff pastry from a local bakery, or a
company like Dufour Pastry Kitchens, in New York City, which makes a terrific product you can order by phone.
Otherwise, the frozen puff pastry you find in your supermarket is perfectly acceptable.

Occasionally, prepared pie shells are deployed and also rolled, stretched, or cut. Other times, finely ground
cookies are used—Lemon Curd Tart with Cookie Crust is made from paper-thin chocolate wafers, and Toasted
Pecan Bars are made from graham cracker crumbs.

You will be hard-pressed to pick which of the eight cookies is your favorite. My husband loves the Cinnamon
Shortbread for its most intriguing texture. I love Moroccan Sandies, made from semolina flour. Most of the cookies,
surprisingly, are flourless.

Marie Gachet's Pillow

8 ounces mascarpone cheese

1 cup all-purpose flour, plus additional for dusting

5 to 6 tablespoons pearl sugar*

This unusual "tea cake" was adapted from a recipe in Food & Wine *magazine by Anne Daguin, the sister of my friend Ariane Daguin. Both are daughters of the famous chef André Daguin. Anne, who owns a bakery in France, found this recipe in an old cookbook written by Marie Gachet, the daughter of Vincent van Gogh's doctor. It really is more cookie than cake, and it "pillows" or puffs as it bakes. Serve the pillow whole and let guests break it into pieces, or make three smaller ones and cut each in half. Great with a proper cup of tea.*

Place mascarpone in bowl of an electric mixer. Stir in the flour and a pinch of salt and mix briefly. Turn the dough out onto a clean work surface, lightly dusted with flour, and knead until smooth. Pat the dough into a 6-inch square and wrap in plastic wrap. Refrigerate 1 hour.

Preheat oven to 450°F. On a lightly floured surface, roll out the dough to make a 13-by-15-inch rectangle. Or divide dough in thirds and roll out into thin circles. Wrap the dough around the rolling pin and unroll onto a large baking sheet. Sprinkle evenly, and heavily, with pearl sugar.

Bake 14 to 15 minutes, until pastry is slightly puffed and golden brown. The sugar will caramelize in patches on the surface. Serve whole or cut in half. Serve warm or at room temperature.

Serves 6

*This is also delightful made with turbinado sugar or rainbow-colored sugar, available in many specialty food and baking stores.

Vanilla Tea Ring

6 extra-large eggs

1¼ cups vanilla-sugar

1⅓ cups self-rising cake flour

This is just the sort of homey (and low-fat!) treat you can whip up for a spontaneous tea party. This cake is also versatile: use it as a base for shortcakes (by sandwiching halved sugar-coated berries between two thin slices); serve it toasted, with homemade jam; or spread it with apple butter, dust it with cinnamon-sugar, and broil until bubbly.

Preheat oven to 350°F.

Separate eggs. You will need 4 yolks and 6 whites. (Save remaining yolks for another use.)

In bowl of an electric mixer, combine egg yolks with 3 tablespoons water. Beat on medium speed and gradually add 1 cup vanilla-sugar. Increase speed to high and continue beating until yolk mixture is thick and pale yellow. Slowly add flour and briefly mix on low speed. Mixture will be stiff. Using a flexible rubber spatula, transfer mixture to a large bowl.

Thoroughly clean bowl of electric mixer, and add egg whites, a pinch of salt, and beat on medium speed until frothy. Slowly add remaining ¼ cup vanilla-sugar and beat until stiff and glossy, being careful not to overbeat.

Add one-quarter of the beaten whites to the yolk mixture and gently mix. With rubber spatula, add remaining whites and fold until just combined, deflating mixture as little as possible.

Coat a heavy 10-inch nonstick bundt pan with nonstick vegetable cooking spray. Pour batter into pan. Bake about 45 minutes, until a wooden skewer inserted in the cake comes out clean. Transfer pan to a rack. Let it cool 30 minutes. Run a small, thin knife around the edges of the cake to loosen. Turn out onto a large plate.

Serves 8 to 10

Meringue Nests with Lime Custard

**3 extra-large egg whites
and 6 egg yolks**

⅞ cup plus ½ cup sugar

4 large limes

Here's a dessert you need to think about preparing as soon as you wake up, since the meringue shells are put into a hot oven in the morning and then left for 12 hours with the oven turned off as you go about your day. No peeking! Then all you need to do is whip up the luscious lime custard about an hour before serving. This is a special dessert for company and tastes a lot like a trip to Key West.

Preheat oven to 400°F.

In bowl of an electric mixer, put egg whites and a pinch of salt. Beat until frothy and slowly add ⅞ cup sugar, 2 tablespoons at a time, until the whites are very thick and glossy. Do not rush this step. The mixture should look like thick marshmallow fluff.

Line a baking sheet with parchment paper. Make 6 large mounds of stiff egg whites and, using the back of a large spoon, smooth into nest shapes, making an indentation for the custard with the back of the spoon. Put in the oven and close the door. Turn oven off. Let meringue stay in oven for 12 hours. Do not open oven!

One hour or two hours before serving, make the lime custard: Grate the rind of enough limes to get 2 tablespoons zest. Set aside. Cut 3 or 4 limes in half and squeeze to get ½ cup juice.

Place 6 egg yolks in a metal bowl over a pot of simmering water, making sure that the bowl does not touch the water. Stir in ½ cup sugar. Using a wire whisk, whisk vigorously while cooking the eggs and sugar, 1 minute. Slowly add lime juice and 1 tablespoon zest. Continue to cook about 5 minutes, whisking constantly, until ribbons form and the mixture is the texture of thick pudding. Do not rush this step either. Remove bowl from heat and let cool 5 minutes, whisking frequently. Cover and refrigerate up to 1 hour.

Fill the dry meringue shells with custard, making sure to smooth the tops. Sprinkle with reserved lime zest. Serve within 1 hour of filling.

Serves 6

Maple Walnut Loaf

8 ounces shelled walnuts (about 2 cups)

2 extra-large eggs, at room temperature

½ cup plus 2 tablespoons pure maple syrup

Just when you think there's nothing to go with a cup of coffee, you can whip (literally) three simple ingredients into a homey cake with a delicate crumb. Serve, if you like, with a scoop of Maple Snow (page 17), fashioned from only one ingredient—pure maple syrup.

Preheat oven to 350°F.

Place walnuts in a large nonstick skillet. Cook over medium heat, stirring constantly, about 5 minutes, until nuts are lightly toasted and have a faint nutty smell. Remove from heat and let cool completely. When the nuts are cool, place in bowl of a food processor and process until finely ground. Set aside.

Pour boiling water into the bowl of an electric mixer. Pour it out, then dry bowl thoroughly. (This warms the bowl, so when you beat the eggs they increase dramatically in volume.) Place eggs, maple syrup, and a pinch of salt in warm bowl. Beat on maximum speed 6 to 7 minutes, until the mixture has thickened and increased in volume.

Using a flexible rubber spatula, gently fold the ground walnuts into egg mixture. Line the bottom of an 8½-inch nonstick loaf pan with parchment paper. Pour mixture into pan.

Bake 40 to 42 minutes, until a wooden skewer inserted in the cake comes out clean. Using a pastry brush, glaze top of cake with remaining maple syrup. Run a small, thin knife around the edges of the cake to loosen. Turn cake out of pan and cool on a rack.

Serves 6 to 8

Note: 8 ounces shelled walnuts equals 2 cups whole or 1½ cups chopped.

Italian Plum Crostata

¾ cup pure maple syrup

2 pounds ripe Italian plums

1 sheet frozen puff pastry dough (about 8¾ ounces)

I look forward to the hazy, lazy end of summer when these little football-shaped plums come to market. They are wonderful eaten out of hand, but are even more delectable in this open-face fruit tart. Wildflower honey can be substituted for the maple syrup.

Put maple syrup in a small saucepan and cook over medium heat until reduced to ½ cup, about 5 minutes. Let cool.

Wash plums and dry well. Remove pits, leaving plums as intact as possible. Place plums in a 4-quart pot. Add all but 1 tablespoon cooled maple syrup and cook over high heat until plums give up much of their liquid and are soft, but still retain their shape. Using a slotted spoon, transfer plums to a coarse-mesh sieve and place over the pot that has the plum-maple liquid. Let drain 1 hour, then pat plums dry.

Preheat over to 400°F.

Meanwhile, defrost pastry dough. Roll out slightly with a rolling pin and fit into a 9-inch removable-bottom tart pan. Prick bottom of pastry several times with a fork. Make sure dough comes up 1 inch above the rim of the pan. Place plums on pastry, pressing down to cover all the spaces. Fold about ½ inch of the pastry over the plums. Using a pastry brush, brush pastry with a little maple syrup.

Place tart in oven and bake 25 to 28 minutes, until pastry is golden. While tart is baking, reduce plum-maple liquid in pot over medium heat until it is thick and syrupy and reduced to about ⅓ cup. If your plums are on the tart side, add a little more maple syrup to the glaze and reduce some more.

Remove tart from oven and place on a rack. Using a pastry brush, lightly brush half of the glaze on plums. Let cool a little and glaze again. Let tart cool completely.

Serves 8

Jam Tart with Powdered Sugar

12 ounces prepared pie dough*

¾ cup best-quality raspberry preserves

6 tablespoons confectioners' sugar

Simple, no-nonsense, and strangely elegant, this is what you prepare when you yearn for something sweet and freshly baked. It has all the flavor virtues of a jelly doughnut without the messy yeast dough and deep-fat frying. I like raspberry jam the best, but you may try those seasonal homemade jams you find at farmers markets; or mix together all those almost-empty jars of jam in your fridge.

Preheat oven to 425°F.

Make sure dough is at room temperature. Roll out half the dough on a clean, dry surface with a rolling pin to make a 10-inch circle. Place on a baking sheet.

Spread preserves on dough, leaving a ¾-inch border all the way around. Roll out the remaining dough to make a 10-inch circle and place on top. Press edges together firmly and then roll up the edges all around to make a tight raised border.

Using a small sharp knife, make several squiggly slits in the top crust. Sprinkle the top (leaving the edges clean) with 3 tablespoons confectioners' sugar pushed through a sieve. Bake about 22 minutes, until jam is bubbly and the edges are golden.

Remove from oven. Let cool. Sprinkle with remaining sugar. Cut into wedges.

Serves 8

*Use good-quality frozen pie crusts, or you can make your own.

Lemon Curd Tart with Cookie Crust

4 cups plain yogurt

32 chocolate wafers

12 ounces best-quality lemon curd

You could use almost any cookie to make an amazing one-ingredient crust, but I've always loved the combination of lemon and chocolate, so Nabisco chocolate wafers work perfectly. Use an imported lemon curd (the Brits make the best) for the most sublime filling. It's an interesting interplay of slightly sour and very sweet.

Line a large sieve with cheesecloth or filter papers and dump in all but 2 tablespoons yogurt. Place sieve over a bowl to catch liquid and refrigerate 4 to 5 hours.

Two hours before serving, preheat oven to 350°F.

Place chocolate wafers in bowl of a food processor. Process until you have fine crumbs. (Optional: Reserve 2 tablespoons crumbs for garnish.) Add reserved 2 tablespoons yogurt and process again. Add 1 to 2 tablespoons water and process briefly until a slightly sticky dough is formed.

Coat an 8-inch removable-bottom fluted tart pan with nonstick vegetable spray. Press in crumb "dough," making sure that the bottom is thoroughly covered. Push the crumbs up the sides of the pans. Bake 16 to 18 minutes, until crust is dry and firm. Let cool 10 minutes. Set aside until ready to fill.

Transfer thickened yogurt to a bowl, discarding all the liquid. Mix yogurt with all but 3 tablespoons lemon curd. Mix thoroughly and refrigerate 1 hour. Fill tart shell with yogurt mixture. Swirl remaining lemon curd on top. (If desired, garnish with reserved 2 tablespoons crumbs.) Serve within 2 hours of filling.

Serves 8

Hazelnut Angel Cake

7 ounces shelled chopped hazelnuts (about 1¾ cups)

1 cup confectioners' sugar

8 extra-large eggs

This heavenly cake is made in an angel food cake pan. Finely ground hazelnuts take the place of flour, and the rest is based on simple technique. Using nuts with the skins on, and toasting them before grinding, intensifies their flavor.

Preheat oven to 350°F.

Place nuts on a baking sheet and bake 6 to 8 minutes, until nuts are golden and lightly toasted. Shake pan several times to prevent burning. Remove from oven and let cool.

When cool, place nuts in bowl of a food processor with 2 tablespoons confectioners' sugar. Process until very fine and powdery. Set aside.

Separate eggs and place 6 egg yolks in bowl of an electric mixer with 2 tablespoons water. Beat on maximum speed, and after 1 minute add ½ cup confectioners' sugar. Continue to beat 3 to 4 minutes, until mixture is very thick and pale yellow. Gently fold ground nuts into mixture. Transfer to a large bowl.

Thoroughly clean mixing bowl, add 8 egg whites and a pinch of salt, then beat on medium speed. Continue beating and add ¼ cup confectioners' sugar. Beat until whites are glossy and stiff. With a flexible rubber spatula, carefully fold whites into nut mixture. Do not overmix.

Coat a 10-inch angle food cake pan with nonstick vegetable spray. Pour mixture into pan, smoothing top with spatula. Bake 45 minutes. Do not open oven door during baking.

Remove from oven and let cake cool in pan on a rack. When cool, remove cake from pan. Sprinkle with remaining 2 tablespoons confectioners' sugar pushed through a sieve.

Serves 8

Dried Fruit Strudel

1 sheet frozen puff pastry dough (about 8¾ ounces)

1 pound mixed dried fruit

½ cup poppy-seed filling*

I don't suggest you run out and purchase a 14-by-4-inch rectangular removable-bottom tart pan to make this recipe, since you can simply roll the filling strudel-style in a rectangle of puff pastry—but if you happen to see one in a kitchenware shop, don't hesitate to buy it. This tart or quiche pan is known in French as moule à flan *or* quiche rectangulaire, *and its unexpected shape makes this simple dessert seem extravagant.*

Place dried fruit in a medium saucepan with 2 cups cold water. Bring to a boil, then lower heat to medium. Cook 15 minutes, or until fruit is soft. Drain well in a colander and let cool 15 minutes.

Transfer fruit to a large cutting board and, using a large chef's knife, coarsely chop the fruit. Mix chopped fruit thoroughly with poppy seed filling. Set aside.

Defrost pastry dough. While still cold, roll it out lengthwise so that it is about 16 inches long and wider than the original width by 4 inches. Cut off a 16-by-4-inch wide piece and refrigerate until ready to use.

Preheat oven to 400° F.

Place larger sheet of pastry in a 14-by-4-inch rectangular tart pan and trim the edges to fit. Make sure that the pastry comes to the top of the pan. Prick the bottom several times with a fork. Refrigerate until ready to use.

Fill pastry with fruit-poppy seed filling, making sure that the mixture fills in all the crevices. Top with refrigerated panel of puff pastry, making sure all of the edges are pressed together, using a little water if necessary to seal. Using a small, sharp knife, make equidistant slits, on the bias, in the top. Bake 35 to 40 minutes, until puffed and golden brown. Let cool.

Serves 8

*Available in cans in the baking section of most supermarkets.

Butterscotch Torte

5 extra-large eggs

9 ounces butterscotch morsels

3 tablespoons plus 1 teaspoon cinnamon-sugar

The texture of this very sweet cake falls somewhere between a wet soufflé and pecan pie. I suggest you serve it in small portions, slightly warm, accompanied by strong espresso.

Preheat oven to 375°F.

Separate eggs. Place yolks in a small bowl and place whites in bowl of an electric mixer.

Place butterscotch morsels in a metal bowl over a pot of simmering water, making sure the bottom of the bowl does not touch the water. Heat until melted, stirring often. Remove from heat and whisk in yolks, stirring with a wooden spoon or rubber spatula until thoroughly incorporated.

Beat egg whites together with a pinch of salt and 3 tablespoons cinnamon-sugar until stiff peaks form. Fold one-quarter of the beaten whites into butterscotch mixture, then fold the remaining whites into mixture.

Coat an 8½-inch removable-bottom cake pan with nonstick vegetable spray and line the bottom with a round of parchment paper. Spray paper lightly. Pour in the batter and sprinkle with 1 teaspoon cinnamon-sugar. Bake 35 minutes. Remove pan from oven and let cool on a rack 15 minutes. Serve slightly warm.

Serves 6 to 8

Glazed Pear and Lychee Tarts

20 ounces canned lychee nuts in heavy syrup

1 sheet frozen puff pastry dough (about 8¾ ounces)

3 large ripe pears

The flavor duet of fresh pears and lychees is fascinating because one seems to magnify the taste of the other. Happily, canned lychee nuts, although not quite as exotic as the fresh ones, are available all year long. They do double duty in this recipe by forming a custardy layer to support the pears, and their liquid gets reduced to a burnishing glaze.

Preheat oven to 400°F.

Drain lychees in a colander over a small heavy saucepan. Press down to extract all the liquid. Pat lychees with paper towels to dry well.

Thaw pastry dough and cut into 4 rectangles, about 4 by 5 inches. Cut ¼-by-4-inch strips from the two ends of each rectangle and place on top of those edges.

Tear lychee nuts in half and place torn side down on top of pastry, leaving the two edges of each tart exposed. Peel pears and cut into very thin wedges or slices. Place pears in a tight, overlapping fashion on top of the lychees, filling in any empty spots.

Place tarts on an ungreased baking sheet (lined with parchment, if you wish) and bake 20 minutes, until edges of pastry have puffed. While tarts are baking, cook lychee liquid over medium heat about 15 minutes, until reduced to a dark amber syrup, about ¼ cup.

Using a pastry brush, glaze the tarts lightly but completely, and bake 10 minutes longer. The pastry will be golden brown. Remove tarts from oven and brush with remaining glaze. Let cool on baking sheet. Serve slightly warm or at room temperature.

Serves 4

Chaussons: Fruit Butter Pastries

**1 sheet frozen puff pastry
dough (about 8¾ ounces)**

**1 cup prune butter, apple butter,
pear butter, or chunky
fruit preserves**

¼ cup cinnamon-sugar

These almost-elegant pastries are a cinch to make even if you've never worked with puff pastry before. They're filled with thick fruit butter—prune (also known as lekvar), apple, pear, apricot, or any other variety you can find. You also can substitute a really chunky fruit preserve—strawberry or mirabelle plum work especially well. These treats look like narrow envelopes with slits that slyly reveal the filling. A simple quenelle of vanilla ice cream turns this into dessert for company. Dust the edges of the plate with more cinnamon-sugar.

Thaw puff pastry dough. Preheat oven to 375°F.

Roll out dough so that it is about 12 inches square. Cut into 6 even rectangles, about 4 inches wide and 6 inches long.

Spread about 2½ tablespoons fruit butter in a wide stripe down the length of each pastry a little to the right of dead center. Sprinkle each with 1 teaspoon cinnamon-sugar. Fold over to make logs that are 2 inches wide and 6 inches long. Press edges tightly together and trim with a small, sharp knife to make neat packages. Make 4 slits ½ inch from edge of pastry, about 1 inch apart, down the length of pastry.

Brush tops very lightly with water. Sprinkle pastries evenly with remaining cinnamon-sugar. Place on an ungreased baking sheet and bake 25 minutes, or until golden. Remove carefully with a spatula and let cool.

Serves 6

Apple Pizza with Cider Glaze and Cider Sorbet

1 quart fresh apple cider (unpasteurized*)

1 sheet frozen puff pastry dough (about 8¾ ounces)

2 very large apples, Red Delicious or a local variety

This is a great dessert when you need something big. With little effort you can serve 8 guests a slice of "pie" and a scoop of sorbet. Apple cider, reduced to a syrup as thick as honey, is used to glaze the fruit; it also gets the cold treatment—simply frozen into an icy granita, or processed into a smoother sorbet.

TO MAKE CIDER SORBET: Put 2 cups cider in an ice cream maker and freeze according to manufacturer's directions. Or put 2 cups cider in a shallow nonreactive dish and place in the freezer. Break up ice crystals with a fork every 30 minutes until cider freezes, about 3 hours. Or freeze in an ice cube tray and process in a food processor (chill the blade of the processor first) until it has the consistency of sorbet.

Preheat oven to 450°F.

Put 2 cups cider in a small nonreactive saucepan. Bring to a boil and lower heat to medium. Cook until thick and reduced to ⅓ cup, about 20 minutes. Set glaze aside.

Thaw puff pastry dough. Place on a large flat baking sheet. Stretch dough gently in all directions to almost cover baking sheet. Trim with a sharp knife to make circle 12 inches in diameter.

Peel and core apples, leaving them whole. Cut into paper-thin slices horizontally (the hole should be in the center of the apple slice). In a tight overlapping fashion, cover all but a ½-inch border of the pastry circle with apple slices, beginning at the outside of the pastry and arranging slices in concentric circles toward the center. Brush apples with the cider glaze and bake 20 minutes, or until golden brown. Remove from oven. Let cool at least 10 minutes. Serve warm or at room temperature with a small scoop of the sorbet.

Serves 8

*Available in the produce section of most supermarkets.

Bourdelots: Pastry-Covered Pears or Apples

5 large ripe seasonal pears or apples

¾ cup plus 2 tablespoons vanilla-sugar

1 sheet puff pastry dough (about 8¾ ounces), chilled

Inspired by Shirley King's charming book Pampille's Table: Recipes and Writings from the French Countryside, *this dessert, generally made with* pâte brisée, *hails from Normandy and is equally satisfying with puff pastry. The better the puff pastry, the more supernal the results, so buy some from a local bakery or gourmet shop, if possible. Make sure the pears are ripe, the apples flavorful.*

Preheat oven to 400°F.

Peel 4 pears or apples and trim the bottoms so that the fruit sits without wobbling. Roll each piece of fruit heavily in vanilla-sugar, being sure to coat completely.

Dust a work surface with vanilla-sugar. Cut pastry dough into 4 squares. With a rolling pin, roll each piece of pastry on sugar to enlarge it 1 to 2 inches on each side. You want the pastry to be thin. Place a piece of fruit in center of each pastry square. Fold pastry over the top of the fruit, making sure the entire pear or apple is wrapped. You may have to gently stretch the dough as you go along. Secure the dough using a little water, if necessary. Press firmly to seal.

Place fruit on a baking sheet. Bake about 30 minutes. Pastry will be golden and sugar will be caramelized. Remove from oven. Let sit 10 minutes before serving.

TO MAKE WITH PEAR OR APPLE PUREE: Peel remaining pear or apple, core, and cut into large chunks. Place in a small saucepan with ¼ cup water and 2 tablespoons vanilla sugar. Bring to a boil. Lower heat and cover. Simmer 10 minutes, or until fruit is soft. Transfer fruit and liquid to a blender and puree until very smooth. Serve warm alongside warm bourdelots.

Serves 4

Strawberry Summer Cake

6 ounces store-bought ladyfingers (24)

2 pounds ripe strawberries

1 cup vanilla-sugar

I call this a summer cake because it is similar to an English summer pudding (which can be made any time of the year and is not actually a pudding—the English call all their desserts puddings). English summer puddings are made with white bread; I have substituted ladyfingers for a more refined look. This is, of course, most sublime in the late spring and summer months when strawberries are at their flavorful best.

Line a 6-quart soufflé dish with plastic wrap, being sure that it overhangs the edge of the dish by several inches.

Split the ladyfingers apart lengthwise horizontally and place, cut side up, to cover bottom of dish. Make sure to fill in any holes. Place a layer of cut ladyfingers around the sides of the dish, standing erect, cut side facing in. Place another layer in the bottom and press down firmly.

Wash strawberries and dry thoroughly. Set aside 6 strawberries with stems. Remove stems from remaining strawberries, cut in half, and place in a large saucepan with sugar. Over high heat, mash with a potato masher until chunky. Bring to a boil. Boil 1 minute. Let cool.

When cool, pour strawberry mixture and all juices into prepared soufflé dish. Top with remaining ladyfingers so that the strawberries are completely covered. Fold plastic wrap over the top of the ladyfingers to make a tight package. Weight the cake down with a saucepan filled with water (making sure the bottom of the pan is the same diameter as the cake and fits directly on top).

Refrigerate 24 hours. Unmold cake onto a large plate and remove plastic wrap. Cut into wedges and garnish with a few of the reserved whole strawberries.

Serves 6

Toasted Pecan Bars

5 ounces graham crackers*

1½ cups chopped pecans

1 cup sweetened condensed milk

This treat is for my dad, the big guy who scored the winning touchdown on New Year's Day in 1942 for the University of Tennessee in the Sugar Bowl. He really loves sweets and he especially loves pecans. You can cut these into small bars as a kind of brownie or into larger squares served slightly warm and topped with vanilla ice cream. There are different kinds of graham crackers on the market, so you can experiment with honey-cinnamon or chocolate flavors.

Preheat oven to 350°F.

Break up graham crackers and place in bowl of a food processor. Process until very fine and powdery. Transfer to a bowl.

Place pecans in a large nonstick skillet over medium heat and cook 5 to 6 minutes, until nuts are toasted and have a nutty smell. Transfer to a cutting board. Let cool a few minutes, then finely chop, using a large chef's knife.

Add pecans to graham cracker crumbs and mix. Add a large pinch of salt and the sweetened condensed milk. Stir until thoroughly mixed. Mixture will be very sticky. Line the bottom of a shallow ovenproof dish, about 12 by 6 inches, or a 9-by-9-inch baking pan, with parchment paper. Coat paper and sides of dish with nonstick vegetable spray. Using a rubber spatula, transfer dough to pan. Wet your hands with cold water and pack dough firmly into baking pan, being sure to smooth the top. Bake 35 minutes. Remove from oven and let cool in pan. Cut into 16 bars.

Makes 16 small bars or 8 large squares

*This is equivalent to 10 graham cracker sheets or 40 crackers. You may substitute 1½ cups ready-made graham cracker crumbs.

Almond Galettes

6 ounces sliced almonds with skins (about 2 cups)

3 extra-large eggs

¾ cup plus 6 tablespoons confectioners' sugar

These individual cakes are extremely pleasing for afternoon tea, served with sweetened whipped cream and fresh strawberries, or as a showy dessert served with freshly made ice cream, or with a glass of sherry. This is a "no-bowl" cake—made in a food processor.

Preheat oven to 350°F.

Spread almonds on a baking sheet and bake until golden brown, about 6 minutes. Shake the pan several times so the almonds don't burn. Remove from oven and let cool completely.

When cool, reserve 3 tablespoons almonds for garnish, and place the remainder in bowl of a food processor. Process nuts until finely ground. Add eggs, ¾ cup confectioners' sugar, and a pinch of salt. Process until smooth.

Lightly coat four 4½-inch removable-bottom tart pans with nonstick vegetable spray. Pour batter into tart pans. Place tart pans on a large baking sheet and bake 18 minutes, or until just set. Remove from oven.

In a small bowl, stir 6 tablespoons confectioners' sugar and 1 tablespoon warm water until completely smooth. Spoon this icing evenly onto each warm galette and spread to make a thin layer. Garnish with the reserved toasted almonds. Let cool and remove from tart pans.

Serves 4

Chickpea Flour Cookies

½ **pound unsalted butter, at room temperature**

1½ **cups confectioners' sugar**

2 **cups roasted chickpea flour,* plus additional for dusting**

I first became familiar with chickpea flour in the south of France, where I attended a cooking school run by Roger Vergé. It is the essential ingredient used for making socca, *an indigenous pizzalike snack, thin and pliable, and blackened from wood-fired ovens. This flour is also used for making fournade, a simple soup from Burgundy, and for* panelle, *little chickpea flour pancakes, familiar in the south of Italy. I became so enamored with the stuff that I started experimenting and now I make all of the above . . . and these addictive cookies. They have a faint nutty taste and a delicate texture. They are an excellent choice for those on a gluten-free diet.*

In bowl of an electric mixer, cream butter until light and fluffy. Add 1 cup confectioners' sugar and cream thoroughly. Stir in chickpea flour and add a pinch of salt. Continue to mix until dough forms a smooth ball. Wrap in plastic wrap and refrigerate 30 minutes.

Preheat oven to 300°F.

Sprinkle pastry board lightly with chickpea flour. Using a rolling pin, roll dough out to ¼ inch thick. Using a cookie cutter, preferably one with fluted edges, cut into desired shapes. Prick each several times with a fork.

Place cookies on ungreased baking sheet. Bake 25 minutes, or until golden. Let cool on baking sheet and then transfer to board.

Sprinkle generously with remaining confectioners' sugar pushed through a sieve. (For visual contrast, you can leave half of the cookies plain, and dust half of the cookies with sugar.) Transfer to a platter.

Makes about 36 cookies

*Available in Middle Eastern markets and specialty food stores. You may also use plain (unroasted) chickpea flour, almond flour, or chestnut flour.

Peanut Thins

1 cup super-chunky peanut butter

1 cup plus 2 tablespoons turbinado sugar*

1 extra-large egg

I might have been the only kid in the neighborhood who hated peanut butter. Even today I think it's an acquired taste. I am, however, very fond of these cookies, inspired by a recipe from Gourmet *magazine. They are oddly sophisticated, with a lovely crisp texture, and go wonderfully with a tumbler of cold apple cider.*

In bowl of an electric mixer, put peanut butter and 1 cup turbinado sugar. Blend until smooth. Add the egg and a pinch of salt and mix thoroughly. Transfer to a large piece of plastic wrap and form into a thick flat disk. Wrap tightly and refrigerate 30 minutes.

Preheat oven to 375°F.

Break off 36 pieces of chilled dough, about 2 teaspoons each, and roll into balls about 1 inch in diameter. Place on a large ungreased baking sheet and, using the tines of a fork, flatten into disks about 1¼ inches in diameter. Sprinkle lightly with remaining 2 tablespoons turbinado sugar.

Bake 14 to 15 minutes, until just firm to the touch. Remove from oven. Let cookies cool on baking sheet. Store in a tightly covered tin.

Makes about 32

*You can also use granulated or light brown sugar.

Moroccan Sandies

1 cup unsalted butter

1⅛ cups confectioners' sugar

2¼ cups semolina flour

The authentic name for these semolina pastry balls is ghoriba mughrabi, *but I have renamed them in honor of their birthplace and their distinctive texture. These improve with age, hour by hour. If they last long enough, you'll discover what I mean. They are made with fine semolina flour, available in Middle Eastern and health food stores, and with clarified butter.*

Melt the butter in a small saucepan over very low heat. Using a spoon, remove all the white foam from the surface. Slowly pour the butter into a large bowl, making sure not to include any of the milky white solids that have accumulated in the bottom of the saucepan. Add 1 cup confectioners' sugar, semolina flour, and a pinch of salt. Mix with a wooden spoon until the mixture is stiff. Add up to 3 tablespoons cold water so that you have a dough that you can knead. It will be very crumbly.

Using your hands, knead the dough in the bowl for several minutes, until smooth. Place dough in a large piece of plastic wrap and form into a large thick disk. Set aside at room temperature for 3 hours.

Preheat oven to 350°F.

Break off 32 pieces of dough, about 1¼ inches in diameter, and roll into perfectly formed balls. You will need to warm up the dough in your hands to make it more pliable; the dough at this point still has a rather crumbly texture. Place balls on a large ungreased baking sheet. Bake 15 minutes, or until firm. Remove from oven and let cookies cool on baking sheet.

When cool, put remaining ⅓ cup confectioners' sugar in a sieve and generously dust the cookies. Store in a tightly covered tin.

Makes 32

Cinnamon Shortbread

½ cup plus 2 tablespoons unsalted butter

2 cups self-rising cake flour

½ cup plus 1 teaspoon cinnamon-sugar

You'll feel so good making these cookies because they look just like the expensive imported ones, right down to the decorative little marks made with the tines of a fork. The idea of using cake flour was somewhat accidental, but the results were irresistible: a refined yet crumbly texture, with an overlay of cinnamon spice and a lick of salt. These improve with age and are scrumptious with a cup of Earl Grey tea.

Preheat oven to 325°F.

Let butter come to room temperature and cut into small pieces. Place flour in bowl of an electric mixer and add ½ cup cinnamon-sugar. Process briefly. Add butter and continue to mix on medium speed until small clumps begin to form. Add 1 tablespoon cold water and continue to mix until the dough comes together in a smooth ball.

Place dough in an ungreased 9-inch pie pan. Press down firmly to make a uniform layer. Using a butter knife, smooth the top. Sprinkle 1 remaining teaspoon cinnamon-sugar on top. Score dough into 16 wedges and then prick each wedge 3 times with a fork.

Bake 40 minutes. Remove from oven. While still warm, cut into wedges with a small, sharp knife. Let cool completely. Store in a tightly covered tin.

Makes 16

Hungarian Nut Cookies

2 cups hazelnuts or walnuts, lightly toasted

2 extra-large egg whites

1 cup packed dark brown sugar

Few cookies are easier to make or more sublime to eat. I created them for my beautiful Hungarian mom, who called them finum, *or refined. Sometimes we eat them with a strong cup of coffee as we play Scrabble, or after dinner, with a slightly chilled glass of sweet Tokay wine.*

Preheat oven to 350°F.

In bowl of a food processor, process nuts until coarsely ground. Set aside.

Place egg whites in bowl of an electric mixer with a pinch of salt. Beat until just beginning to stiffen. Add brown sugar and beat until stiff peaks form and the mixture is glossy. Carefully fold in nuts with a flexible rubber spatula.

Line a baking sheet with parchment paper. Drop heaping tablespoons of batter onto parchment. Bake 20 minutes, or until cookies are dark beige and just set.

Remove from oven and let cookies cool on baking sheet. Remove with spatula, and store in a tightly covered tin.

Makes 24

Soft Raisin Cookies

½ pound marzipan

3 extra-large egg yolks

Scant ½ cup raisins

You'll never guess that the base of these soft, yielding cookies is marzipan. The almond-based confection provides the structure, but not the flavor, of the dough. You can use black or yellow raisins, sun-dried cranberries, or even chopped dates. Be sure not to substitute almond paste for marzipan because they behave quite differently—the almond paste will hold its ball shape rather than relaxing into a flat cookie. Also, it is much more intense in flavor.

Preheat oven to 375°F.

In bowl of an electric mixer, beat marzipan until soft and smooth. Add a pinch of salt and egg yolks, one at a time, beating well after each addition. Stir in raisins.

Drop 12 heaping tablespoons, about 2 inches apart, onto a parchment-lined baking sheet. Bake 18 to 20 minutes, until golden. Optional: Five minutes before the end of baking, beat 1 additional egg yolk with 1 teaspoon water. Using a pastry brush, lightly glaze cookies and bake 3 minutes longer. Remove from oven and let cool on baking sheet. Remove with a spatula.

Makes 12

Halvah Chip Cookies

½ pound marbled halvah, coarsely crumbled

1 extra-large egg yolk plus 1 whole egg

⅔ cup semisweet chocolate chips

The haunting flavor of this cookie comes from halvah, a ground-sesame sweetmeat from the Middle East. You can use any of a variety of halvahs from marbled to pistachio, and you can use mint chocolate or white chocolate chips. Oil-rich halvah produces a cookie that is both moist and crisp and looks just like, but tastes quite different from, your run-of-the-mill chocolate chip cookie.

In bowl of an electric mixer, beat halvah and egg yolk until soft and smooth. Add whole egg and beat until smooth. Fold in chocolate chips and stir until thoroughly mixed. Dough will be sticky. Place bowl with dough in refrigerator about 20 minutes.

Preheat oven to 375°F.

Line a baking sheet with parchment paper. Drop tablespoons of dough onto baking sheet. If desired, press a few chips into tops of cookies. Bake 20 minutes. Remove from oven and let cookies cool on baking sheet. Remove with a spatula.

Makes 14

Gianduia Sandwich Cookies

1 cup Nutella

1 extra-large egg

**1 cup self-rising cake flour,
plus additional for dusting**

Be sure to use self-rising cake flour for these delectable sandwich cookies with their European schmear of creamy Nutella, a chocolate-hazelnut spread that also flavors the simple-to-make batter. Gianduia is the Italian name of a chocolate-hazelnut confection, and also is the name for that particular flavor combination.

Preheat oven to 375°F.

In bowl of an electric mixer, put ½ cup Nutella and the egg. Mix well. Slowly add 1 cup flour until a wet dough is formed. Dust a board with a little more flour and transfer dough to board. Knead gently, adding a little more flour if necessary. Dough will be sticky. Roll dough into 18 balls, flouring your hands as you go to make rolling easier, and place on parchment-lined baking sheet, several inches apart.

Bake 12 minutes. Let cool 10 minutes. Using a serrated knife, split cookies in half horizontally. Spread bottom with 1 teaspoon Nutella, then replace top, pressing firmly. Let cool completely. Store in a tightly covered tin.

Makes 18

Really Nice Sugar Cookies

½ cup unsalted butter

¾ cup all-purpose flour,
plus additional for dusting board

¼ cup sugar,
plus additional for sprinkling

What gives these simple, dimpled cookies their incomparable taste and texture is the use of browned butter, also known as beurre noisette. *Unsalted butter is melted in a saucepan and cooked until the butter smells nutty and is brown in color. The browned butter is then chilled until firm so that it can be incorporated into a fine cookie dough. Although my son Jeremy is a little too old to groove on an entire plate of homemade cookies (and they really don't go with beer), I still make these when he comes to visit.*

Place butter in a small, heavy saucepan and melt over medium heat. Cook 4 to 5 minutes, until butter is browned. Let cool. Transfer butter, being sure not to include the blackened bits, to a small bowl. Refrigerate until firm, about 4 hours.

In bowl of a food processor, process flour, sugar, and a pinch of salt. Add the chilled butter in tiny pieces. Add 1 tablespoon cold water and process just until dough comes together. Wrap in plastic wrap and refrigerate 1 hour.

Preheat oven to 375°F.

Lightly flour a board and roll out dough ⅛ to ¼ inch thick. Using a small round cookie cutter, about 1½ inches in diameter, cut out 18 circles. Place circles on a parchment-lined baking sheet and sprinkle very lightly with a little more sugar.

Bake 14 to 15 minutes, until golden and just firm. Remove from oven. After 3 minutes, make an indentation in center of each cookie with your thumb. Let cool on sheet.

Makes 18

1-2-3 Cake, Cookie, and Tart Ideas

Try "snitz," or dried apple pie. Soak dried apples in water. Mash together with some vanilla-sugar and cook 5 minutes. Place in a pie pan lined with flaky pie dough. Cover with top crust and sprinkle with more vanilla-sugar, making a few slits. Bake at 375°F., 30 minutes.

Make a simple pie dough. Place 2 cups flour, 7 tablespoons cold unsalted butter, 2 teaspoons sugar, and pinch of salt in a food processor. Pulse 10 seconds and add 7 to 8 tablespoons cold water. Knead on floured board and chill 1 hour before rolling out.

Great for dunking, try sweet zwieback. Beat 2 eggs together with ⅔ cup vanilla-sugar and 1 cup flour. Bake in a small loaf pan at 400°F. for 25 minutes. Slice and bake on a baking sheet 10 minutes.

Make your own sweet turnovers. Cut chilled puff pastry dough into 6-inch squares and fill with crumbled halvah and golden raisins, or with raspberry jam and almond paste. Fold over into triangular shapes and bake at 400°F., 12 minutes, or until golden.

Cut puff pastry dough into a 10-inch square and line with long, thin oval slices of banana, leaving a ½-inch border. Glaze with melted apricot jam and bake 25 minutes.

Make pithiviers—a double-crust puff pastry tart. Cook dried apricots in water until soft and lightly caramelized. Roll out two 12-inch circles of chilled puff pastry dough. Place cooked apricots on one circle and crumble marzipan on top. Cover with second circle, press edges together, and trim edges to form a perfect circle. Bake at 400°F. for 30 minutes, and cut into wedges.

Try cinnamon-sugar grissini. Buy very thin breadsticks and brush with melted butter. Roll heavily in cinnamon-sugar. Bake on baking sheet at 350°F., 10 minutes.

Make "cookies-while-you-sleep." Beat 3 egg whites together with a pinch of salt and 1 cup sugar until thick and glossy. Fold in chocolate chips, butterscotch chips, chopped pecans, or any combination. Drop by spoonfuls on parchment-lined baking sheet. Place in preheated 400°F. oven and turn oven off. Let sit in oven 12 hours.

Make cocoa clouds. Preheat oven to 250°F. In bowl of an electric mixer, beat 6 egg whites, 6 tablespoons cocoa powder, and 6 tablespoons superfine sugar. Beat until stiff peaks form, drop spoonfuls onto parchment-lined baking sheet, and bake 1 hour.

Try *puits d'amour* ("wells of love" by baking small round puff pastry shells. Dust with confectioners' sugar and fill with seedless raspberry jam or red currant jelly.

Make little nut cakes. Process 2 cups toasted almonds in a food processor with 1 cup superfine sugar, 2 eggs, and 2 yolks to make a batter. Pour into 12 muffin tins lined with paper liners and place 1 whole almond in center of each. Bake at 325°F., 25 minutes.

For elegant sugar crisps. Preheat oven to 400°F. Brush wonton wrappers with melted butter. Sprinkle with vanilla-sugar or cinnamon-sugar. Bake 5 minutes, or until crisp.

Make sweet lime meringues. Beat 2 egg whites together with ⅓ cup confectioners' sugar, 1 tablespoon grated lime zest, and 1 teaspoon lime juice until glossy and stiff. Pipe through a pastry bag onto parchment-lined baking sheet. Bake at 225°F. until dry.

For quick almond macaroons. Place ½ pound almond paste in a food processor and add 1 cup sugar and 2 egg whites. Process until smooth. Pipe through a pastry bag onto parchment-lined baking sheet. Bake at 325°F., 18 minutes.

Chocolate

FEW WORDS PROMPT INSTANTANEOUS PLEASURE LIKE "CHOCOLATE."

No doubt you already are smiling and experiencing the little rush of anticipation that only a chocolate truffle can provide. Linnaeus, the Swedish botanist who developed a system to classify plants in the eighteenth century, assigned the cacao tree to a botanical genus he affectionately named Theobroma, "food of the gods."

There is great connoisseurship when it comes to chocolate. Everyone has a preferred style—milk chocolate, bittersweet, or semisweet; and a childhood favorite—brownies, mousse, pudding; and grown-up fantasies—soufflés, fondues, and pots de crèmes. You will find them all in this chapter, including chocolate truffles.

Chocolate contains phenylethylamine, a chemical responsible for the euphoric feelings associated with romance, and a wealth of beneficial antioxidants—far beyond that of blueberries or broccoli. (Dark chocolate has twice the amount as milk chocolate.) So there is much to love.

Many of the following recipes require melting chocolate. It must be done slowly, in a bowl over simmering water or in a microwave oven (see page 141), so that it does not "seize up" or get hard or grainy.

Another factor in the success of a recipe has to do with the chocolate itself. Most of my recipes were initially made with the semisweet chocolate you can get at the supermarket, because I believe that everyone ought to be able to make this panorama of treats affordably and spontaneously. But then I experimented with some of the super-premium chocolates available today and experienced a layer of complexity and richness that was, well . . . transcendent, possessing the winy virtues of a great Bordeaux. My favorites include Scharffen Berger chocolate from California and Michel Cluizel chocolate from France.

What to drink with chocolate desserts? Some experts believe that Cabernet Sauvignon and chocolate are a great team. But I don't agree. There is not enough residual sugar and too much tannin in good Cabernets to stand up to the sweetness and heftiness of most chocolate desserts. Instead try a glass of Malmsey Madeira; a ruby port from a good producer; a voluptuous recioto della Valpolicella—a sweet red wine from Italy; or a dark and raisiny Malaga wine. My husband likes bourbon with chocolate. For me, there is nothing better than a shot of espresso.

Since chocolate is the single most craved food in this country, this might be the most sought-after chapter.

Chocolate Demitasse with Amaretto and Soft Whipped Cream

12 ounces best-quality milk chocolate, in one piece

1½ cups heavy cream

6½ tablespoons amaretto

If you want to end your special dinner on a high note, make this. Serve instead of dessert, instead of coffee, or as an elegant coda after coffee.

Grate 2 tablespoons chocolate on small holes of box grater. Refrigerate until ready to use. Coarsely chop remaining chocolate and put in a heavy saucepan. Add 1 cup cream and cook, over medium heat, until chocolate melts. Add 5 tablespoons amaretto, reduce heat to low and cook, stirring, until mixture is smooth and thick.

Meanwhile, in bowl of an electric mixer, whip remaining ½ cup cream until it begins to thicken. Add remaining 1½ tablespoons amaretto and whip briefly until stiff peaks form.

Ladle chocolate mixture into 6 demitasse cups. Spoon whipped cream over each and sprinkle with grated chocolate. Serve immediately.

Serves 6

Dark Chocolate Mousse

4 extra-large eggs

8 ounces good-quality semisweet chocolate

3 tablespoons Kahlúa

Not every recipe should be stripped to its skivvies, but this is a pure and simple mousse, just the way I like it. It is dark and sensual, and in my opinion would be burdened by the cream, sugar, and butter often found in other versions. Kahlúa, a rich coffee-flavored liqueur from Mexico, adds wonderful harmonics to the bass note of chocolate. You can substitute Tía Maria or another dark coffee liqueur.

Separate eggs. Put yolks in a small dish and whites in the bowl of an electric mixer.

Chop chocolate into small pieces. Place chocolate in top of a double boiler or in a bowl over simmering water, making sure bowl doesn't touch water. Melt chocolate completely, stirring occasionally with a wooden spoon. Stir in yolks and continue to stir until glossy and smooth. Slowly add Kahlúa and stir vigorously. Switch to a small wire whisk and continue to cook and whisk the mixture until it is hot to the touch and is quite thick.

Beat the egg whites together with a pinch of salt until glossy and stiff.

Remove chocolate mixture from the heat and let cool about 5 minutes. Fold the stiff whites into the chocolate mixture until thoroughly incorporated. Spoon mousse into 4 wine glasses or dessert coupes. Cover and chill several hours. This can be made a day in advance. Let sit at room temperature about 10 minutes before serving. Garnish with shaved chocolate, if desired.

Serves 4

Mint Chocolate and
White Chocolate *Pots de Crème*

2 cups heavy cream

7 ounces dark mint chocolate or white chocolate

4 extra-large egg yolks

Pots de crème *refers simultaneously to a sultry custard and to the lidded cups in which they are baked. You can make the mint chocolate or white chocolate version of this—the world's most heavenly dessert—or you can make them both for drama. In either case, you will find that the results are worth the effort and the calories.*

Preheat oven to 325°F.

Heat cream in a heavy saucepan until it just comes to a boil. Chop chocolate into small pieces and add to cream. Stir constantly until chocolate is completely melted and mixture is smooth.

Beat egg yolks in bowl of an electric mixer until pale yellow, 3 to 4 minutes. A little at a time, pour hot cream mixture over eggs, beating constantly until all the cream is incorporated.

Pour mixture into six 5-ounce pots de crème cups or ramekins. Place cups in a deep baking dish and carefully add boiling water so that it comes almost all the way up the sides of the cups or ramekins. Bake 25 to 28 minutes, until barely set.

Remove cups from water bath. Let cool, then refrigerate several hours, until cold. Let sit at room temperature 15 minutes before serving. Garnish with chocolate leaves or chocolate curls (page 141).

Serves 6

Chocolate Aspic
with Whipped Cream

1¾ cups heavy cream

**8 ounces best-quality
semisweet chocolate**

**2 packages unflavored gelatin,
about 1½ tablespoons**

I have never eaten, seen, or heard of chocolate aspic, so what better reason to invent one? It took many tries to get it right. Make sure to serve this at room temperature because that's when its magical texture emerges—when both the gelatin and chocolate loosen their grip.

Heat 1½ cups cream in a small heavy saucepan until just boiling. Add chocolate, lower heat to medium-high, and stir constantly until chocolate is completely melted and smooth, about 3 minutes. Remove from heat.

Put 2 cups cold water in a large mixing bowl. Sprinkle gelatin over water and let sit 1 minute, then stir until gelatin dissolves.

Heat chocolate mixture over high heat until it just comes to a boil. Stirring constantly, slowly pour very hot chocolate mixture into bowl with dissolved gelatin and water. Mix with a wooden spoon 5 minutes, until gelatin is completely incorporated.

Coat six 5-ounce timbales or custard cups with vegetable cooking spray and pour mixture in. Or pour into champagne flutes or small wine glasses. Chill until set, about 3 hours.

Let sit at room temperature for 30 minutes to 1 hour before serving. When ready to serve, whip remaining cream until firm. Turn aspic out from molds (loosen the sides with a small sharp knife or dip the molds into several inches of hot water), and serve with whipped cream. Or mound champagne flutes or wine glasses with cream, smoothing the top.

Top with chocolate curls (page 141), or other chocolate garnish, if desired.

Serves 6

Chocolate Yogurt with Prunes

½ **pound large pitted prunes (about 24)**

6 ounces semisweet chocolate

2 cups plain yogurt

My dear friend Rona Jaffe, the best-selling author, doesn't know how to cook. Yet sometimes she comes up with food ideas that make you smile. She sprays Pam on pasta, and melts chocolate into yogurt, which she then sprinkles with turbinado sugar. The chocolate-yogurt thing gave me the idea for this dessert, and it tastes like rich, thick, slightly tart chocolate pudding. The prunes add body and soul.

Cut prunes into small pieces and place in a bowl. Cover with boiling water and let sit 15 minutes. Drain well and pat completely dry.

Place chocolate in top of a double boiler or in a bowl over simmering water, making sure bowl doesn't touch water. Stir constantly until the chocolate melts completely. Remove from heat and gradually whisk yogurt into chocolate. Whisk until the chocolate is incorporated and the mixture is very smooth.

Place some of the chocolate mixture in the bottom of 4 wine glasses. Add some prunes. Top with a layer of the chocolate mixture then the remaining prunes. Cover with remaining chocolate mixture. Chill until very cold.

Serves 4

Chocolate-Rhubarb "Pudding"

10 ounces semisweet chocolate in one piece, or 8 ounces chocolate chips

2 pounds trimmed rhubarb

1 cup sugar

This dessert was a happy accident. It was early spring and I wanted to use all the beautiful crimson rhubarb available in my local farmers' market. I began with rhubarb and sugar, naturally, but never did I imagine that the leftover chocolate chips in my freezer would make a pudding that was this irresistible. I still can't decide whether I like it better warm, straight from the pot, or chilled, when the pudding thickens and becomes creamy and mysterious. Your guests will wonder what the three ingredients could possibly be.

If you are using a single piece of chocolate, let it come to room temperature so you can make decorative chocolate curls. Using a sharp vegetable peeler, make long thin curls of about 2 ounces of the chocolate and set in a cool place to harden. Coarsely chop the 8 ounces remaining chocolate and set aside.

Cut rhubarb into 1-inch pieces. Put in a saucepan with sugar and 2 cups water. Cook over medium-high heat 10 to 15 minutes. Do not stir. Cook until rhubarb has softened, then stir and add chopped chocolate or chocolate chips. Continue to stir until chocolate has melted and is thoroughly incorporated. Transfer to 4 wine glasses. Let cool to room temperature. Garnish with chocolate curls or chocolate leaves (page 141). Or, before filling glasses, simply dip the edges of the glasses into a dish of water, about ¼ inch deep, and then dip into a saucer of sugar. Let harden a few minutes, then fill with chocolate mixture. The pudding is also delicious served cold.

Serves 4

Ultra-Light Chocolate "Brownies"

6 large eggs

9 ounces good-quality semisweet chocolate

½ cup confectioners' sugar

There are very few chocolate recipes using real ingredients—pure chocolate, eggs, and sugar—that fit into the low-calorie category. These do. Got skim milk?

Preheat oven to 350°F.

Separate eggs. Beat yolks in bowl of an electric mixer 5 minutes, or until thick and pale yellow. Fold warm chocolate into egg yolks. Set aside.

Chop chocolate and place in top of a double boiler or in a bowl over, but not touching, simmering water. Stir frequently until smooth.

Using clean beaters, whip egg whites together with sugar and a pinch of salt. Whip until stiff peaks form. Fold one-fourth of the whites into chocolate mixture to lighten, then fold in remaining whites. Mix thoroughly.

Coat a 9-by-9-inch baking pan with vegetable cooking spray. Pour in batter. Bake 22 to 24 minutes, until just set but still a little soft in the center. Loosen the edges with a sharp knife. Cool cake on a rack. Cover pan tightly with foil until ready to serve. Cut into 12 squares. Dust with additional confectioners' sugar.

Serves 12

Chocolate Meringue Cake

5 extra-large eggs

1 cup vanilla-sugar

12 ounces best-quality semisweet chocolate

This multilayered chocolate cake supports crisp, airy disks of chocolate meringue frosted with a thick chocolate paste—made in the style of zabaglione—with egg yolks that are beaten and cooked in a double boiler, then tempered with gobs of melted chocolate. The result is a surprising refinement of the French cake known as dacquoise.

Preheat oven to 275°F.

Separate eggs. Put whites in bowl of an electric mixer. Add a pinch of salt and slowly add vanilla-sugar, beating until glossy and stiff.

Chop 4 ounces chocolate and place in a small heavy saucepan. Melt over very low heat. Cool 2 minutes. Add chocolate to egg whites and gently mix. Line three 9-inch pie pans with rounds of parchment paper in bottom of pans. Evenly divide chocolate mixture among pans, making a thin layer. Bake 60 to 70 minutes, until layers are dry and crisp. Remove meringues from oven. Let cool.

Chop 6 ounces of the remaining chocolate into small pieces. Place in a small heavy saucepan and slowly melt over very low heat. Keep warm.

Put egg yolks in top of a double boiler over, but not touching, simmering water. Add 2 tablespoons water and beat several minutes with a whisk to cook yolks slightly and to increase the volume. Working quickly, add melted chocolate to beaten yolks and fold in gently. Set filling aside.

Carefully remove one meringue layer from the pan, peel off the parchment, and place on a cake plate; top with one-third of the filling; place another meringue layer on top and ice with another third of the filling; finish with the last meringue layer and smooth the remaining filling on top with a flexible metal spatula. Let cool.

Grate the remaining 2 ounces chocolate on the large holes of a box grater. Or make chocolate curls or chocolate leaves (page 141). Garnish top of cake. Serve the same day.

Serves 8

Chocolate Fondue with Coconut Cream and Sweet Cherries

1 pound sweet red and/or white cherries

¾ cup plus 2 tablespoons cream of coconut, chilled

8 ounces best-quality bittersweet chocolate

Here's a chance to use one of those popular super-premium dark bittersweet chocolates, such as Scharffen Berger, which is produced in California. Great bittersweet chocolate adds complexity and winy undertones to this suave fondue; cream of coconut adds a voluptuous mouthfeel and a slightly mysterious perfume. Fleshy sweet cherries are the ideal accompaniment because they come with stems for easy dipping and they pair particularly well with dark chocolate. When cherries are not in season, strawberries, bananas, pears, pineapple, peaches, or grapes will do quite nicely.

Wash cherries and dry well. Do not remove stems. Chill until ready to serve.

Put ½ cup cream of coconut in top of a double boiler. Coarsely chop chocolate and add to double boiler. Cook over medium heat but do not stir until chocolate begins to melt. Then stir, using a small rubber spatula, and continue stirring until chocolate melts and a smooth sauce forms. Slowly add ¼ cup cream of coconut.

Transfer chocolate mixture to a small fondue pot or pour into a soufflé dish. Drizzle fondue with 2 tablespoons cream of coconut. Serve with the cherries for dipping. (The fondue can be made ahead of time and reheated in a double boiler.)

Serves 4 or more

Chocolate Delicato

**1 pound chocolate
crunch candy bars***

1 cup cold unsalted butter

**7 extra-large eggs,
at room temperature**

Before I made this cake for the first time, I had an idea of what the results would be and prematurely named my invention "Chocolate Crunch Cake." Nothing could be more misleading—this cake turned out to be light and delicate, with a big surprise: a layer of genoise formed around a firm flanlike center, and those little bits of crunch seemed to melt away. I love this cake and find it most "delicato."

Preheat oven to 425°F.

Line the bottom of a 9-by-3-inch removable-bottom cake pan with a round of parchment paper or aluminum foil. (Make sure the cake pan seals tightly; it will sit in a water bath, and you don't want any leakage.) Coat inside of pan with vegetable cooking spray. Cover the bottom and outside of pan with a single large layer of foil.

Chop candy bars into pieces. Cut butter into small pieces. Place candy bars and butter in a large bowl over a pot of simmering water until chocolate and the butter have melted; make sure bottom of the bowl does not touch the water. Stir frequently with a rubber spatula until smooth. Remove from heat.

Meanwhile, place eggs in bowl of an electric mixer and add a pinch of salt. Beat 6 to 7 minutes, until soft peaks form.

Gradually whisk the chocolate mixture into the eggs.

Pour batter into prepared pan and cover top of pan tightly with a piece of foil that has been lightly sprayed with cooking spray, placing sprayed side down. Place cake pan in a large, deep pan and add enough boiling water to reach the level of the batter. Bake 45 to 50 minutes, until the cake looks as if it's just set. The top of the cake will be soft and slightly spongy to the touch.

Remove cake from water bath and remove the foil. Cake will continue to set as it cools. Let cool 1 hour. Serve, or refrigerate for later use. Let cake come to room temperature before serving.

Optional: Melt an additional 12 ounces of crunch candy and spoon evenly on top of cake. Let harden.

Serves 12

*Use Nestlé's Chocolate Crunch or Cadbury Krisp bars.

Michael's Chocolate Obsession

**1 pound very-best-quality
semisweet chocolate**

10 tablespoons unsalted butter

5 extra-large eggs

This is for hard-core chocolate lovers. You know who you are. The cake tastes extraordinary when faintly warm, about an hour after baking. If serving later, refrigerate, then let come to room temperature. Michael, my husband, recommends a glass of aged port alongside: He thinks it magnifies the chocolate flavor. "After all," he says, "too much ain't enough."

Preheat oven to 375°F.

Line an 8-inch springform pan with a round of parchment paper or aluminum foil. Coat inside of pan with vegetable cooking spray.

Chop chocolate into pieces. Cut butter into small chunks. Place chocolate and butter in top of a double boiler or in a bowl over simmering water, making sure bowl doesn't touch water. Melt, stirring frequently until smooth.

Whisk eggs with an electric mixer together with a pinch of salt, until mixture triples in volume, about 6 minutes.

Fold chocolate mixture into egg mixture with a flexible rubber spatula, until completely incorporated.

Pour mixture into prepared pan. Bake 20 minutes. The center will still be a little soft. Remove from oven. Let cool at least 30 minutes before cutting. You can refrigerate the cake up to 2 days; let sit at room temperature at least 1 hour before serving.

Serves 10

Warm Chocolate Soufflé, Bittersweet Chocolate Sorbet

15 ounces bittersweet chocolate

⅞ cup plus 3 tablespoons vanilla-sugar, plus additional for dusting

5 extra-large eggs, at room temperature

You'll feel like a genius when you serve this impressive chocolate duet. Even more impressive: both the sorbet and soufflé can be prepped early in the day. The sorbet is adapted from Pierre Hermé, one of the world's renowned pastry chefs.

TO MAKE THE SORBET: Chop 6 ounces of the chocolate into small pieces. Put in a heavy saucepan with ⅞ cup of the vanilla-sugar and 1¾ cups water. Cook over medium-high heat until the mixture comes to a boil, about 10 minutes. Boil 2 minutes, stirring constantly. Pour into a small bowl and immediately set into a larger bowl filled with ice cubes. Stir often to cool, and then refrigerate until cold. Freeze in an ice cream maker according to the manufacturer's directions.

TO MAKE THE SOUFFLÉ: Preheat oven to 400°F. Coat four 1-cup ramekins (about 3 inches wide and 2 inches high) with vegetable cooking spray and dust heavily with vanilla-sugar, making sure to coat the bottom and sides. Place on a baking sheet.

Separate eggs. Put yolks in a small bowl and place whites in bowl of an electric mixer.

Chop remaining 9 ounces chocolate and put in double boiler or a large metal bowl set over a pan of boiling water, making sure bowl does not touch water. Melt, stirring frequently until smooth. Remove from heat. Stir yolks into lukewarm chocolate mixture and stir until well blended. Set aside.

Beat egg whites together with 3 tablespoons vanilla-sugar and a pinch of salt until stiff. Fold one-quarter of the egg whites into lukewarm chocolate mixture. In two batches, fold in remaining whites. Divide mixture among prepared ramekins. Run your thumb around the inside edge of each ramekin to wipe clean.

Bake now or cover and refrigerate for up to 12 hours. Bake soufflés until puffed and dry on top; the inside should be moist. This will take about 12 to 13 minutes if the soufflé is at room temperature, or about 15 to 16 minutes if the soufflé has been refrigerated.

Serve immediately with sorbet alongside in small dishes or small chilled glasses.

Serves 4

Rich Chocolate Pudding

2½ cups milk

6 ounces semisweet chocolate or chocolate chips

3 tablespoons cornstarch

I don't know why anyone wouldn't make chocolate pudding from scratch—unless they didn't know how! After quite a bit of experimentation, I offer you this simple and sublime rendition. This is delicious warm, right from the pot, and great cold, too.

Put 2¼ cups milk in a saucepan. Chop chocolate into small pieces and add to saucepan. Cook over medium-high heat, stirring constantly, until chocolate melts and the mixture comes just to a boil.

Put remaining ¼ cup milk in a small cup and add cornstarch. Stir to dissolve. Slowly add dissolved cornstarch to hot milk, whisking constantly, and cook over medium heat 2 to 3 minutes. The milk will thicken into a creamy pudding. Remove from heat and spoon into 4 wine glasses or small dessert bowls. Cover each with plastic wrap. Serve at room temperature or chill until cold.

Serves 4

Chocolate-Pepper Truffles

8 ounces semisweet chocolate chips

½ cup heavy cream

½ cup Dutch cocoa powder

These unusual truffles are heavily laced with black pepper and "sweetened" with a pinch of salt. Contrary to what you might think, salt accentuates the sweetness of chocolate. Composed of the stuff you should always have on hand, you can make these at the drop of a hat, when surprise guests drop in.

Place chocolate chips in a small heatproof bowl.

Put cream in a saucepan and bring to a boil. Pour cream over chocolate in bowl and stir constantly until chocolate melts. (If it doesn't completely melt, place heat-proof bowl in a shallow bowl of boiling water and stir.) Add a large pinch of salt and scant ½ teaspoon freshly ground black pepper. Stir and refrigerate, about 45 minutes until just firm enough so that you can roll mixture into balls.

Roll chocolate into small balls, about ¾ inch in diameter. Put cocoa powder on a plate and roll balls in cocoa to cover completely. Serve immediately or place on a plate and refrigerate until firm.

You can roll in more cocoa before serving. Let sit at room temperature 30 minutes. Serve on a doily-lined plate or in individual 1-inch fluted paper cups.

Makes 20 to 24

Little Chocolate-Sesame Cups

½ cup dried currants

8 ounces good-quality semisweet chocolate

¼ cup tahini (sesame-seed paste)

While working on a Hanukkah story for Gourmet *magazine, I invented these wonderful little candies quite out of desperation. I wanted to make chocolates to go with a dessert of baked oranges, but many chocolate candies use butter or cream, which were not permissible for my kosher meal. So I substituted tahini (sesame-seed paste) with astonishing results; studded with plumped currants, these taste like beloved Chunky bars.*

Place currants in a small bowl with boiling water to cover. Let sit 5 minutes. Drain and pat dry with paper towels.

Coarsely chop chocolate. Stir tahini until smooth. Put chocolate and 3 tablespoons tahini in top of a double boiler or in a bowl over simmering water, making sure bowl does not touch water. Stir until chocolate is melted and tahini has been incorporated. When mixture is completely smooth, stir in currants.

Spray eighteen 1-inch candy paper liners with vegetable cooking spray. Spoon chocolate mixture into cup liners and let cool 5 minutes.

Decorate candies by dipping tip of a toothpick into the remaining tahini and swirling it into tops of candies. Chill until set. These will keep, covered and refrigerated, for 1 week.

Makes 18

Chocolate Cream
and Raspberry Parfait

2½ pints big ripe raspberries

**2 cups sour cream
or crème fraîche**

**10 ounces semisweet
chocolate, coarsely chopped**

This recipe is short on prep time and a great example of the less-is-more style of entertaining. The synergy of chocolate, berries, and acidity from the sour cream makes the whole more than the sum of its parts—it tastes like one big chocolate-covered cherry. It's perfect for a spontaneous dinner party when you want something da morire *(to die for)!*

Wash raspberries and pat completely dry. Chill until ready to use.

Put sour cream in a small saucepan and bring just below a boil, whisking often. Immediately add chocolate and remove from heat. Stir constantly until chocolate is completely melted.

Gently fold in 2 pints raspberries. Using a long spoon, carefully distribute mixture among 6 small glasses or champagne flutes. Garnish with remaining raspberries and refrigerate for at least 2 hours before serving.

For added drama, you can dollop some sour cream on top.

Serves 6

Pecan-Fudge Terrine

½ heaping cup coarsely chopped pecans

⅔ cup sweetened condensed milk

6 ounces semisweet chocolate, chopped

This is a great little candy you can whip up for your kids or serve to company. For the kids, pour the warm mixture into a square pan, then cut into small pieces when chilled. For company, pour the mixture into a small terrine, or loaf pan, and serve in elegant slices with coffee.

Place pecans in a small nonstick skillet and add a large pinch of salt. Cook over medium heat, stirring constantly, until nuts are toasted. Set aside to cool.

Put condensed milk in a small saucepan. Heat until it just comes to a boil and add chocolate. Immediately lower heat and stir until blended. Continue to cook, over low heat, stirring constantly, about 1 minute, until chocolate has completely melted. Stir in pecans and cook a few seconds. Pour the warm mixture into a 7-by-7-inch square pan. (If you wish, sprinkle the top with ¼ cup additional chopped toasted pecans.) Or line a 3-by-5-inch loaf pan with plastic wrap so that it hangs over the pan and pour in the mixture. (It will not come up to the top of the pan.) Fold plastic wrap over chocolate and press firmly to smooth the top. Refrigerate until cold.

Let sit at room temperature 5 to 10 minutes, then cut into squares or slices.

Makes 16 squares or 20 slices

Chocolate Half-Moons

12 round wonton wrappers, chilled

⅓ cup Nutella (chocolate-hazelnut spread)

2 tablespoons unsalted butter

These are unexpectedly hip petits fours to serve with coffee or an after-dinner brandy. Made from round wonton wrappers, they are filled with chocolate-hazelnut spread and folded over. My friend Danny Young, a journalist and cookbook author who lives in Paris and New York, makes a larger version of these anytime he wants to seduce a date. You can also make "blintzes" by substituting egg roll wrappers.

Place wonton wrappers on a large board. Working quickly, put a heaping teaspoon of Nutella in center of each wonton. Dip your finger in a small bowl of cold water and wet the perimeter of the wonton. Fold over to make a half-moon shape. Press edges tightly together. Press down lightly on top of folded wonton to spread the chocolate mixture and flatten slightly. Repeat with remaining wonton wrappers and Nutella.

Melt butter in a large nonstick skillet. When the butter is hot (be careful not to let the butter brown), add wontons. Cook about 2 minutes on each side, or until the wontons are golden and crisp. Serve hot.

Makes 12

1-2-3 Chocolate Ideas

Shower curls of dark or white chocolate over prunes that have been poached in a sweet red wine such as recioto della Valpolicella or Banyuls.

Stuff plump, moist dried dates with almond paste and dip in melted bittersweet chocolate.

Insert a thin slice of candied ginger into a small slit made in a giant strawberry, preferably one with a long stem. Dip in melted white chocolate.

Make chocolate-raspberry turnovers. Cut puff pastry into rectangles and place a small piece of milk chocolate and some raspberry jam in center. Fold in half and bake. Drizzle the tops with a little melted chocolate.

Make an unusual watermelon and chocolate salad. Thinly slice very ripe watermelon and splash with crème de cassis. Shower with shards of dark or white chocolate.

Glaze plain store-bought cakes. Boil together 1 cup heavy cream and ½ cup light corn syrup. Pour the mixture over 12 ounces chopped bittersweet chocolate and stir until smooth. Pour over pound cake or angel food cake and spread with an offset metal spatula.

Toast a piece of country bread and top with a little salted butter and a thin slice of good chocolate. Or try it the Dutch way: butter a thick slice of brioche and coat heavily with chocolate sprinkles.

Make homemade nonpareil candies: Spoon small rounds of melted dark chocolate, flavored with a little orange oil, onto parchment paper. Sprinkle with white or silver dragées.

Melt dark chocolate and fold into mascarpone cheese. Flavor with dark rum and use as a dip for cookies or fruit.

Make s'mores. Sandwich toasted marshmallows and melted chocolate between graham crackers.

Try Jacques Torres's Chocolate Rice Crispies. Melt dark chocolate together with heavy cream and fold in Rice Krispies. Spoon into small mounds and let harden.

Enjoy a chocolate truffle cake. Melt 1 pound chocolate and let cool slightly. Fold into 1 quart whipped heavy cream and pour into a 10-inch cake pan lined with plastic wrap. Chill several hours, then unmold. Dust with cocoa powder.

Make white chocolate–peppermint candies for the holidays. Melt 8 ounces white chocolate together with 2 tablespoons white crème de menthe. Spread in a 7-by-7-inch pan and press ¼ cup crushed peppermint candies into top. Chill and cut into squares.

Working with Chocolate

TO MELT CHOCOLATE:
Method 1: Chop dark, milk, or white chocolate into small uniform pieces. Place in a metal bowl over 1 to 2 inches very hot or just simmering water. Do not let the bottom of the bowl touch the water. Any water or moisture that comes in contact with the chocolate will make it seize up and become hard and grainy and therefore not usable. You can melt chocolate with a little bit of liquid (liqueur, butter, and so on), but never add it midway, only in the beginning. Be patient. I have ruined a lot of chocolate in my time.

Method 2: I don't own a microwave, but according to master pastry chef Pierre Hermé, it's a good way to melt chocolate: Place the chopped chocolate in a microwave-safe container. Cook on medium for 1 minute, stir the chocolate, and continue to cook for 30-second intervals, until melted. If you're melting more than 4 ounces of chocolate, you can start at 2 minutes and then go to shorter intervals. Keep checking, because the chocolate keeps its shape even though it's melted. (Adapted from *Desserts by Pierre Hermé,* Little, Brown, 1998.)

TO MAKE CHOCOLATE LEAVES:
Wipe 20 lemon or other leaves clean, and pat dry. Line a baking sheet with aluminum foil. Melt 4 ounces semisweet chocolate in the top of a double boiler over simmering water, stirring occasionally until smooth. Remove from heat and spread a thin layer of chocolate over veined side of leaves. Place on prepared sheet. Refrigerate until firm, about 30 minutes. Gently peel leaves off chocolate, starting at stem end.

TO MAKE CHOCOLATE CURLS:
Bring a block of white or dark chocolate to warm room temperature, 75° to 80°F. The chocolate is ready when the surface is slightly oily. Using a wide vegetable peeler, dig lightly into the chocolate and pull toward you to make curls. If chocolate is too warm, it will not curl. If it's too cold, you will get chocolate shavings instead of curls. Place on parchment-lined baking sheet until ready to use.

Ice Creams and Frozen Desserts

ICE CREAM UNLEASHES A CHILDLIKE INNOCENCE IN ALL OF US. IT IS OUR REWARD at the end of a day. We respect its simplicity and love its possibilities. At the very least, it puts us in good humor.

If you lined up a spoonful of each of the frozen treats in this chapter you would have more than twenty colors, textures, and flavors. There are coarse-crystalled granitas and smooth ices; refined sorbets and creamy sherbets; semifreddo; and ice cream fantasies like Lemon Melting Moments, Cinnamon Ice Cream with Cinnamon Brittle, and Ice Cream Profiteroles with Mint Chocolate Sauce.

Many of these selections do not require special equipment, but to experience the full range of possibilities, now's the time to invest in an ice cream machine. You can buy a very inexpensive manual ice cream maker from Donvier, or the slightly more expensive electric version from Cuisinart. You can buy an old-fashioned hand-cranked machine that requires rock salt and ice for freezing and lots of friends, or go the more professional route with the Simac "Gelataio." With all ice cream makers, however, one factor ensures success: the ice cream mixture or base must be very cold before churning.

The remarkable food writer Elizabeth David, produced a four-hundred-page social history of ice cream and ices entitled *Harvest of the Cold Months* (Viking Penguin) that chronicles the development of our affection for frozen desserts, beginning with the earliest recorded ice houses in Mesopotamia, almost four thousand years ago, to uncovering the links between Levantine sherbets and the sorbets and ices of Europe. It's a worthwhile read while the particles of your ice cream or sorbet aerate and slowly freeze into scoops of pleasure.

Since these frozen treats use only three ingredients, their flavors are pure and intense. Ripe fruit, good chocolate, and patience are prerequisites to the process. But once you've mastered the art of making ice cream, it is sure to become child's play.

For extra pleasure, I've devised vibrantly flavored sauces to drizzle, spoon, or pour upon your favorite store-bought or homemade ice creams. Five of the sauces use ice cream itself as one of the ingredients! If you lined up a spoonful of each, you would have ten colors, textures, and flavors. Consider the possibilities.

Lemon Melting Moments with Candied Lemon Rind

4 large lemons

⅔ cup plus ¼ cup sugar

8 extra-large eggs

Here's a luxurious frozen soufflé that tastes like ultra-creamy ice cream but doesn't require an ice cream maker. Instead, the mixture is made like a mousse: whipped egg whites are folded into lemony custard, and then frozen. For a crowning touch, you can top each soufflé with a web of glistening candied lemon peel.

Grate the rind of enough lemons to get 1½ tablespoons zest. Cut lemons in half and squeeze juice to get ⅔ cup. Set aside.

Separate eggs. You will use 3 whites. (Save remaining whites for another use.)

Place yolks in a metal bowl and stir in ⅔ cup sugar. Place over a pot of simmering water, making sure the bottom of the bowl does not touch the water. Cook yolks and sugar 1 minute, whisking constantly. Slowly add lemon juice and zest and continue to cook 4 to 5 minutes, whisking constantly until airy and very thick. Remove from heat.

In bowl of an electric mixer, beat 3 egg whites together with a pinch of salt until frothy. Slowly add ¼ cup sugar and beat until very thick. Fold the yolk mixture into the stiff egg white mixture and blend thoroughly using a flexible rubber spatula.

Wrap four 6-ounce ramekins with a double layer of aluminum foil so that the foil wraps tightly around the ramekin and comes up at least 2 inches above the rim. Spoon custard mixture into ramekins, filling as much as possible. Place ramekins in freezer for several hours. Remove foil before serving.

To make candied lemon peel: Using a small sharp knife, remove long panels of rind from 3 additional lemons. Remove all the white pith and cut the rind into long, very thin strips using a sharp knife or scissors. Blanch strips in boiling water 3 minutes. Discard water, then bring fresh water to a boil and blanch strips again for another 3 minutes. Drain, then return peel to a small saucepan with ½ cup water and ¼ cup additional sugar. Cook 10 minutes over medium-high heat until lemon peel is glazed. Let cool and serve atop soufflés.

Serves 4

Champagne and Melon Ice

3½ cups champagne

2½ cups sugar

3 cups diced melon

My dear friend Ilene Shane was Ralph Lauren's private chef for seven years, catering every sort of party and celebration imaginable. Her stylish repertoire of original recipes runs from simple to elaborate, and are the ultimate in taste and refinement. Here's an example.

In a shallow dish that will fit easily in the freezer, put champagne, 2 cups sugar, and ¼ cup water.

Put melon in bowl of a food processor and coarsely puree on the pulse setting. Stir melon puree into champagne mixture to combine thoroughly. Freeze for at least 6 hours or overnight.

Wet the rims of small wine glasses or martini glasses with water and dip in remaining sugar. Shave the frozen melon mixture with the edge of a large spoon and place in glasses. Serve immediately. Decorate with little paper umbrellas used for tropical mixed drinks.

Serves 8

Granita al Caffe

3 cups hot brewed espresso or flavored coffee

⅓ cup plus ½ tablespoon sugar

½ cup heavy cream

This slushy jolt of caffeine is admired in Italy, where it is served as a snack. In Sicily one enjoys it in the morning, sometimes scooped into a sweet brioche. For an American variation use a flavored coffee, brewed double-strength (hazelnut or vanilla or chocolate-raspberry), and top with rainbow-colored sugar to make you smile. Serve with a glob of sweetened whipped cream, known in Italy as panna.

Place hot coffee in a medium bowl. Add ⅓ cup sugar and stir until sugar is completely dissolved. Cool to room temperature. Transfer to a shallow metal pie pan and place in the freezer. Every 30 minutes, using a fork, break up ice crystals until mixture is uniformly granular. Continue to freeze and break up ice crystals until frozen, about 3 hours.

When ready to serve, whip heavy cream and ½ tablespoon sugar until thick. Spoon granita into chilled wine glasses and top with whipped cream. Sprinkle a little ground coffee on whipped cream, if desired.

Serves 4 or more

Tangerine-Almond Ice
with Pomegranates

10 large tangerines

½ cup orzata (almond syrup)*

1 large or 2 small pomegranates

This is a lovely colorful dessert for fall, when the leaves on the trees turn scarlet and orange. Serve with any of the cookies found on pages 110–113. Arrange them on a platter lined with washed and dried autumn leaves. (For Halloween, try the Gianduia Sandwich Cookies, on page 115, for an orange and brown color-coordinated treat.)

Grate the rind of enough tangerines to get 1 teaspoon zest Cut 6 tangerines in half and squeeze to get 2 cups juice. Place tangerine juice, zest, and orzata in a metal pie pan. Place in the freezer. After an hour, using a fork, break up ice crystals. Continue to do so every hour until mixture is frozen solid, about 3 hours.

Peel remaining tangerines and separate into segments. Place segments in a bowl. Cut pomegranate in half and carefully remove seeds with a spoon. Add seeds to bowl with tangerines and chill.

When ready to serve, place chilled tangerine segments and pomegranate seeds in 4 dessert dishes. Break up frozen ice into chunks and place in bowl of a food processor. (Note: It's a good idea to chill the blade and bowl of food processor in the freezer before processing ice.) Process until frozen mixture is smooth.

Place scoops of ices on top of fruit, sprinkle with additional pomegranate seeds, if desired, and serve immediately.

Serves 4

*This is a milky almond syrup, also known as orgeat, available at specialty food stores. Do not substitute the clear almond syrup meant for flavoring coffee.

Lemon Granita
with Sweetened Sour Cream

4 or 5 large lemons

1 cup sugar

1 cup sour cream

Lemon granita is a classic in the repertoire of Italian desserts, and sometimes it's served with whipped cream, which for me hits an incompatible milky flavor note. What's different about this one is its "on key" slather of sour cream, lightly sweetened with sugar and flecked with lemon zest.

Using a small, sharp knife, cut 6 long strips of lemon rind, making sure not to include any white pith. Grate the zest of 1 lemon on medium holes of a box grater to get 1 teaspoon. Set aside. Cut lemons in half and squeeze to get 1 cup juice.

In a heavy saucepan put 2 cups water and all but 2 tablespoons sugar. Bring to a boil. Lower heat to simmer, add lemon juice, and stir until sugar is dissolved. Add strips of lemon rind and let liquid cool.

When cool, strain mixture through fine-mesh sieve. Put mixture in a metal pie pan and place in freezer. Every 30 minutes, using a fork, break up ice crystals until mixture is uniformly granular. Continue to freeze and break up ice crystals until frozen, about 3 hours.

Put sour cream in a small bowl and add remaining 2 tablespoons sugar. Stir until sugar is dissolved. Add 1 teaspoon lemon zest and stir.

Spoon granita into chilled wine glasses. Top with sweetened sour cream and serve immediately.

Serves 6

White Zinfandel-Raspberry Granita

2½ pints ripe raspberries

1¼ cups sugar

1 (750-ml) bottle white Zinfandel

I can't think of a reason to drink it, but white Zinfandel has just the right amount of sweetness and mystery to make a fashionable granita. If you prefer, make this with an off-dry rosé champagne. You can stir the mixture until it is frozen and granular, or you can freeze the mixture overnight and scrape the ice into slushy opal crystals.

Wash raspberries and carefully pat dry. Place 2 pints of the raspberries, the sugar, and ¼ cup water in a medium saucepan. Bring to a boil, stirring constantly to dissolve the sugar. Remove from heat and cool. Transfer a food processor and process until smooth.

Strain the puree through a coarse-mesh sieve into a large bowl. Stir in the wine. Transfer mixture to 1 or 2 metal pie pans and place in the freezer. Every 30 minutes, using a fork, break up ice crystals until mixture is uniformly granular. Continue to freeze and break up ice crystals until mixture is frozen, about 3 hours. Spoon mixture into chilled wine or martini glasses and garnish with remaining raspberries.

Serves 6

Spiced Wine Granita

3 cups full-bodied red wine

½ cup sugar

1 tablespoon mulling spices or pickling spices

This slush is for adults only, since the alcohol from the wine will not evaporate after the brief amount of cooking required. Use a full-bodied red wine such as Merlot or a red wine with good fruit such as a Beaujolais. If you use mulling spices, the mixture will be sweetly aromatic; pickling spices will add verve.

Put wine, sugar, and spices in a small heavy saucepan. Bring to a boil. Reduce heat to low and simmer 6 to 7 minutes. Immediately strain liquid through a fine-mesh sieve. Let cool.

Transfer spiced wine to a metal pie pan and place in the freezer. Every 30 minutes, using a fork, break up ice crystals until mixture is uniformly granular. Continue to freeze and break up ice crystals until frozen, about 3 hours.

If desired, dip the rims of chilled glasses into water and then into sugar and let set until sugar hardens. Spoon granita into glasses. Serve immediately.

Serves 6

Mango-Ginger Sorbet

2 very ripe mangoes, about 8 ounces each

1 cup sugar

4-inch piece fresh ginger

This is scrumptious made with ripe cantaloupe or any other sweet orange-fleshed melon, but the texture of the mango provides the suavest result. Even if you get Chinese takeout, why not provide the dessert to go with the fortune cookies?

Peel mangoes using a small, sharp knife, carefully navigating around the pit. Cut the flesh into small pieces.

In a small saucepan, combine sugar and ¾ cup water. Bring to a boil and simmer until sugar dissolves. Let sugar syrup cool.

Peel ginger and grate on large holes of a box grater. Put grated ginger in a double layer of paper towels and squeeze to extract 2 tablespoons juice.

Place mango, sugar syrup, and ginger juice in bowl of a food processor. Process until very smooth. Cover and refrigerate until very cold. Freeze in an ice cream maker according to the manufacturer's directions.

Serve in chilled ice cream coupes. Garnish with thin slices of additional mango, if desired.

Serves 6

Double Raspberry Sorbet

⅔ cup confectioners' sugar, plus additional for dusting

6 ounces fresh raspberries plus 6 ounces for garnish

10 ounces frozen raspberries in syrup, thawed

Pure berry, pure pleasure—especially if you've had the joy of picking your own berries. Garnish with raspberries that still have their beautiful little green leaves attached and dust the sorbet and raspberries with freshly fallen confectioners' sugar.

Place ⅔ cup confectioners' sugar and ½ cup water in a small saucepan and bring to a boil. Simmer 2 minutes, then remove from heat. Let sugar syrup cool.

Wash fresh raspberries and pat dry. Put 6 ounces raspberries in bowl of a food processor and process until smooth. Add thawed raspberries with all juices and ¼ cup water. Process until very smooth. Place contents in coarse-mesh sieve over a large bowl. Let sit 10 minutes, then press down on solids to extract all the liquid.

Add sugar syrup to raspberry puree and chill until very cold. Freeze in an ice cream maker according to the manufacturer's directions. Scoop into chilled champagne glasses. Garnish with remaining berries and dust generously with confectioners' sugar.

Serves 4

Tropical Coconut Sorbet with Pineapple Syrup

1 (15-ounce) can cream of coconut

2¾ cups unsweetened pineapple juice

4 large limes

You may not be able to immediately identify all three ingredients in this snowy white sorbet, but you will love its tropical intensity.

Place cream of coconut in bowl of a food processor and process briefly until smooth. Remove 2 tablespoons and set aside. Add ¾ cup pineapple juice and ¼ cup water to processor. Squeeze enough limes to get ½ cup juice and add to processor with a pinch of salt. Process until mixture is very smooth. Transfer to a bowl and cover. Refrigerate until very cold. Freeze in an ice cream maker according to the manufacturer's directions. Keep in freezer until ready to serve.

Place remaining 2 cups pineapple juice and 2 tablespoons cream of coconut in a small saucepan. Bring to a boil. Lower heat to a simmer and cook until reduced to ½ cup, whisking often, about 20 minutes. Let cool.

Serve scoops of sorbet with pineapple syrup poured on top. Garnish with thin slices of lime, if desired.

Serves 4

Watermelon Ices with Chocolate "Seeds"

4 cups diced ripe watermelon

¾ cup sugar

½ cup miniature chocolate chips

The riper the watermelon, the more pleasurable this simple dessert. It is easily transmutable: switch the chips for grated lime zest and juice, or for a bracing splash of frozen flavored vodka or melon liqueur.

Remove any seeds from watermelon. Put watermelon in bowl of a food processor and process until very smooth. Add sugar and a pinch of salt and continue to process until sugar is dissolved.

Transfer mixture to a metal pie pan and place in the freezer. After 30 minutes, using a fork, break up ice crystals so that they are uniformly granular. Continue to break up ice crystals every hour until mixture is frozen, about 3 hours.

When ready to serve, chill bowl and blade of food processor. Break frozen mixture into chunks and place in bowl of food processor. Process until very smooth. Spoon the ices into chilled wine or martini glasses and sprinkle with chocolate chips. Serve immediately.

Serves 4

Strawberry Sorbet with
Strawberry Salad, Big Sugar Crisp

2¾ pounds ripe strawberries

½ cup plus 6 tablespoons vanilla-sugar

3 egg roll wrappers*

This is the 1-2-3 philosophy at its apex. Three ingredients; three desserts in one! If you want to add a fourth dimension, make a fresh strawberry syrup by cooking more strawberries with vanilla-sugar in a covered saucepan over low heat for 15 to 20 minutes, then strain through a coarse-mesh sieve. If you want to keep the recipe rolling, add leftover mashed strawberries before making the sorbet, and start again.

Remove stems from 1 pound strawberries. Wash and pat dry. Place strawberries in a food processor with 1 cup water. Add ½ cup vanilla-sugar and a pinch of salt. Process until smooth. Strain through a coarse-mesh sieve and chill until cold. Freeze in an ice cream maker according to the manufacturer's directions.

When ready to serve, reserve 6 strawberries with stems and set aside. Remove stems from remaining strawberries. Wash and dry well. Cut each strawberry into thin wedges. Distribute strawberries equally among 6 large wine goblets. Sprinkle each with 1 teaspoon vanilla-sugar. Let sit until some juices begin to flow.

Meanwhile, preheat oven to 400°F. Slice each egg roll wrapper in half, diagonally, to make 2 triangles each. Place on a baking sheet. Using a pastry brush, lightly brush each triangle with water. Sprinkle each triangle with 2 teaspoons vanilla-sugar. Bake 5 to 6 minutes, until golden and crisp. Remove from oven.

Top each mound of berries with a scoop of sorbet. Stick a sugar crisp into each scoop of sorbet. Garnish with a berry with stem. Serve immediately.

Serves 6

*Available in packages in the refrigerated or frozen section of Asian food stores and many supermarkets.

Frosted Limes
with Pepper-Lime Sherbet

10 large limes

¾ cup sugar

2½ cups buttermilk

The dominant flavors of this unusual tastebud teaser come from lots of grated lime zest, heady with essential oils, and bits of black pepper. You can serve tiny amounts of this sherbet as a palate cleanser between courses of a fancy meal.

Set 6 limes aside for later. Grate the rind of the remaining limes to get 2 tablespoons zest. Cut in half and squeeze to get ½ cup juice.

In a medium nonreactive bowl, put sugar, zest, and lime juice. Mix well. Add buttermilk, a pinch of salt, and 1 tablespoon coarsely cracked black pepper. Stir until sugar is dissolved. Taste. You want a balance of sour and sweet flavors. Add a little lime juice, if needed. Chill well. Freeze in an ice cream machine according to the manufacturer's directions.

Cut a ⅛-inch "hat" off the tops of reserved limes, saving the tops.

With a paring knife, cut out most of the pulp of each lime, and then, with a small spoon, scrape the remaining pulp from the sides and discard. If necessary, cut off small slices from bottoms so that limes can stand upright. Turn upside down on paper towels to drain.

Fill each shell with sherbet, mounding 1 inch over top of shell. Cover with "hat." Freeze until ready to serve. Let sit 10 minutes before serving, if too hard.

Serves 6

Maple Ice Cream

1 cup milk

⅔ cup pure maple syrup, plus additional for drizzling

1½ cups heavy cream

A lustier extension of the one-ingredient Maple Snow recipe on page 17 is maple ice cream, especially remarkable under a veil of more maple syrup.

Put all ingredients in a large saucepan with a pinch of salt. Bring just to a boil, then lower heat and cook 1 minute, stirring constantly. Remove from heat and let cool. Cover and refrigerate until very cold.

Freeze in an ice cream maker according to the manufacturer's directions. Spoon into chilled dessert coupes. If desired, drizzle with additional maple syrup.

Serves 6

Fresh Melon Gelato

1 large ripe melon (about 2½ pounds)

⅔ cup sugar

¾ cup heavy cream

I was nineteen and in Italy the first time I tried melon gelato, and fondly remember the unexpected interplay of cream and highly perfumed fruit. Gelato, the past participle of the Italian verb gelare, *"to freeze," is used primarily for dairy-based mixtures. This gelato is great—made with Crenshaw, cantaloupe, pink honeydew, Galia, Cavaillon, canary, or casaba melon. Garnish with cubes, balls, or little skewers of whichever variety you choose—just be sure it's fragrant and ripe.*

Remove rind and seeds from melon and cut three-quarters of the melon into small pieces. You should have about 1 pound. Place melon, sugar, and a pinch of salt in bowl of a food processor and process until very smooth.

With motor running, add cream and stop the processor immediately after cream is added. If you overprocess, the mixture will curdle. Transfer mixture to a bowl. Cover and refrigerate until very cold. Freeze in an ice cream maker according to the manufacturer's directions.

Serve scoops of ice cream with little balls or cubes of melon, or with skewers of melon.

Serves 6

Lemon Buttermilk Ice Milk

2 cups superfine sugar

6 large lemons

1 quart buttermilk

This is one of the most frequently requested recipes of the many hundreds I have created! For those who don't own Recipes 1-2-3, *where this recipe first appeared, here it is: a low-fat, frozen treat that tastes a lot like cheesecake.*

Put the sugar in a medium bowl. Grate the rind of 2 or 3 lemons to get 2 tablespoons zest. Squeeze as many lemons as needed to get ½ cup lemon juice. Add zest and juice to the sugar in the bowl and mix until the sugar dissolves.

Whisk in the buttermilk and add a pinch of salt. Stir until sugar is dissolved. Cover and chill several hours. Freeze in an ice cream maker according to the manufacturer's directions.

Serves 8

Frozen Coffee Terrine
with Marsala-Soaked Fruit

16 ounces low-fat coffee yogurt

1¼ cups sweet Marsala

12 ounces mixed dried fruit (a combination of apricots, apples, pears, prunes)

This is a lovely dessert that you will serve from autumn right through winter. The contrast of warm fruit and slowly melting yogurt, gently spiked with sweet Marsala, will surely impress any adult sitting around your table. Consider this for a healthy ending to your Thanksgiving or Christmas dinner, and make it especially impressive by flambéing it with a large spoonful of Marsala.

Place yogurt in a sieve lined with cheesecloth or paper towels and place over a bowl to drain for 15 minutes. Transfer yogurt to a bowl and stir in 4 tablespoons Marsala. Line a small loaf pan or decorative mold with plastic wrap and spoon yogurt mixture into pan. Freeze for at least 3 hours.

Cut fruit into pieces. Place in a large saucepan with ¾ cup Marsala and 3 cups water. Bring to a boil, and boil 2 minutes. Lower heat to medium and cook 10 minutes, or until fruit is soft but still retains its shape. Add ¼ cup Marsala and let cool 15 minutes.

Spoon fruit and juices into 4 flat soup plates. Unmold the frozen yogurt terrine and cut into thick slices. Place 2 slices on each serving of fruit. Garnish each with a few pieces of fruit. Serve immediately.

Serves 4

Vanilla Ice Cream

2 cups half-and-half

**4 extra-large egg yolks,
at room temperature**

½ cup vanilla-sugar

You can make vanilla ice cream with eggs or without, but eggs provide the voluptuous body and mouthfeel that makes us love ice cream as much as we do. If you've never made ice cream before, this is the way to get started.

Place half-and-half in a small heavy saucepan with a pinch of salt and bring just to a boil. Reduce heat and simmer 2 minutes, then cover and remove from heat.

In bowl of an electric mixer put egg yolks and begin to beat. Slowly add sugar and beat until yolks are very pale yellow and thick, about three minutes. While still beating, slowly add warm half-and-half and blend thoroughly. Do not overbeat. Return mixture to saucepan and bring just below a boil; do not boil or mixture will curdle. Immediately lower heat and whisk constantly until mixture thickens and heavily coats a wooden spoon, about 5 minutes Remove from heat and cool, stirring frequently.

Cover and refrigerate until very cold. Freeze in an ice cream maker according to the manufacturer's directions.

Serves 4

Dark Chocolate Ice Cream

2 cups half-and-half

½ cup sugar

**8 ounces bittersweet
or semisweet chocolate**

I dedicate this recipe to my long-time friend Nancy Arum, who has had an outstanding career in the food biz—restaurateur, journalist, ice cream junkie, and author of Ice Cream and Ices *(1981)—and now she has the enviable job of director of sales for the highly acclaimed Scharffen Berger chocolate makers from California. Use their 70 percent bittersweet chocolate for this fabulously simple recipe.*

In a medium saucepan, put half-and-half, sugar, and a pinch of salt. Bring just to a boil, then immediately lower heat to a simmer. Stirring constantly, simmer several minutes, until sugar is completely dissolved. Remove from heat. Cover and keep warm.

Coarsely chop chocolate and place in a double boiler, or in a metal bowl set over simmering water. Make sure bowl does not touch the water. Stirring frequently, melt chocolate until smooth. Slowly whisk in warm half-and-half mixture and continue to cook, whisking constantly, until the ingredients are thoroughly combined. Remove from heat. Let cool. Cover and refrigerate until very cold. Freeze in an ice cream maker according to the manufacturer's directions.

Serves 6

Chocolate Semifreddo

7 ounces semisweet chocolate

1 cup vanilla yogurt

2 extra-large eggs, separated

Semifreddo is a classic dessert from the Veneto region of Italy, but my unusual version uses yogurt as its base to produce the requisite half-frozen texture and accidental taste. It's tangy, it's fun, it's easy to make.

Chop chocolate and put 4 ounces in a metal bowl over a pot of simmering water. Make sure that the bottom of the bowl does not touch the water. Cook over low heat, stirring frequently, until chocolate melts.

Whisk in yogurt and stir just to combine. Add egg yolks and continue to whisk mixture over moderate heat 5 to 6 minutes, until mixture has thickened. The mixture should thickly cover the back of a wooden spoon. Remove from heat and let cool.

In bowl of an electric mixer, beat egg whites together with a pinch of salt until stiff. Fold whites into cooled chocolate mixture. Do not overmix, but make sure whites are thoroughly incorporated.

Line 4 custard cups or dessert molds with plastic wrap. Spoon in mixture and freeze at least 3 hours. Remove from freezer about 15 minutes before serving. Unmold semifreddo onto large plates.

In a small skillet, put remaining 3 ounces chocolate and ¼ cup water. Cook over medium-high heat, whisking vigorously until chocolate melts. Simmer several minutes until thick and creamy. Drizzle semifreddi with warm or room temperature chocolate sauce.

Serves 4

Orange Ice Cream
with Orange-Caramel Sauce

1½ cups half-and-half

1 cup sugar

3½ cups freshly squeezed orange juice

The flavors of this yummy ice cream mimic the Creamsicle of our youth—that block of vanilla ice cream enrobed with orange sherbet, thoughtfully frozen on a stick so you could eat it without a spoon. My version requires a spoon, which is a good thing because you'll not want to miss one bit of the orange-caramel sauce. Squeeze your own oranges for ultimate satisfaction, but when fresh oranges are expensive or not up to par, you can successfully substitute good-quality store-bought juice.

Put half-and-half in a saucepan with ¾ cup sugar and a pinch of salt. Bring just to a boil, whisking constantly. Remove from heat and let cool.

Whisk in 3 cups orange juice and chill until mixture is very cold. Freeze in an ice cream maker according to the manufacturer's directions.

Make orange-caramel sauce by placing remaining ¼ cup sugar in a small nonstick skillet. Cook over medium-high heat until sugar turns into a dark amber liquid. Carefully add remaining ½ cup orange juice. Mixture will bubble up and sugar will harden, but continue cooking over medium heat and hardened sugar will melt. Continue to cook until sauce is reduced to 6 tablespoons. Let cool.

Serve ice cream topped with orange-caramel sauce. If desired, serve in large scooped-out oranges.

Serves 4

Ice Cream Profiteroles
with Mint Chocolate Sauce

**1 sheet frozen puff pastry
dough (about 8¾ ounces)**

**2 pints best-quality
vanilla ice cream**

6 ounces mint chocolate chips

These ice cream puffs are made from store-bought puff pastry instead of the pâte à choux *(a slightly spongy pastry made from butter, flour, and eggs) generally used for profiteroles and éclairs. When ready to serve, spoon the warm mint chocolate sauce over the top of each profiterole.*

Preheat oven to 400°F.

Thaw pastry dough and, while still cold, cut out 12 small circles, using a 2-inch cookie cutter. (Save remaining dough for another use or make more profiteroles.) Place pastry circles on a parchment-lined baking sheet. Bake 15 minutes, or until pastry is puffed and golden brown. Remove from oven and let cool on baking sheet.

When completely cool, split puffs in half horizontally. Reserving ⅓ cup ice cream for making sauce, place a small scoop of remaining ice cream on bottom half of each profiterole and cover with the top half. Place on a plate, cover with waxed paper, and freeze until hard.

Place chocolate chips and reserved ⅓ cup ice cream in a small saucepan. Simmer over low heat and whisk until chocolate is melted and sauce is smooth. Keep warm.

Place 3 filled profiteroles in center of each of 4 large chilled plates. Pour sauce evenly over them. Serve immediately.

Serves 4

Cinnamon Ice Cream
with Cinnamon Brittle

1 cup heavy cream

1 cup milk

**7 tablespoons cinnamon-sugar,
plus 6 tablespoons for
cinnamon brittle**

This is a very professional-tasting ice cream, especially with its crunchy addition of caramelized sugar that hardens into candy. Chop it finely into a thousand amber beads, then make a choice: fold it into freshly churned ice cream or sprinkle generously on top.

Put cream, milk, and 7 tablespoons cinnamon-sugar in a saucepan. Add a pinch of salt and whisk together. Bring just to a boil, then lower heat to a simmer. Simmer 2 to 3 minutes, whisking constantly. Remove from heat and let cool. Cover and refrigerate until very cold. Freeze in an ice cream maker according to the manufacturer's directions.

TO MAKE CINNAMON BRITTLE: Line a board with aluminum foil or use a marble slab. Put 6 tablespoons cinnamon-sugar in a small nonstick skillet and cook over medium-high heat, stirring frequently, until sugar melts into a smooth liquid caramel. Pour hot caramel in a very thin layer onto prepared board or marble. Allow to harden completely. Using a large chef's knife, finely chop into small pieces. Fold into soft ice cream or sprinkle on top.

Serves 4

Roasted Strawberry Ice Cream with Strawberry Compote

2 pints ripe strawberries, plus 2 more pints for compote

1¼ cups sugar, plus ⅓ cup for compote

2 cups heavy cream

Roasting strawberries is a simple technique that makes this strawberry ice cream special. Their natural juices are released, tinting the ice cream a lovely pink and intensifying their inherent flavor. Serve under a coverlet of strawberries and sugar.

Preheat oven to 450°F.

Wash 2 pints strawberries and thoroughly pat dry. With a small, sharp knife, remove stems from 1⅓ pints of strawberries so they won't wobble. Place them cut side down in a metal pie pan. Sprinkle with 1 tablespoon sugar. Place in oven and roast 15 minutes.

Meanwhile, put cream in a small heavy saucepan with 1 cup sugar and a pinch of salt. Bring just to a boil, then lower heat and simmer 2 minutes, stirring constantly, until sugar dissolves. Remove from heat, cover, and keep warm.

Finely chop ⅔ pint strawberries and put in a bowl with 3 tablespoons sugar. Toss and set aside to let sugar dissolve.

Place roasted strawberries and all their juices in a bowl of a food processor. Add warm cream and process until almost smooth. Transfer to a bowl and fold in chopped strawberries and all their juices. Cover and refrigerate until very cold. Freeze in an ice cream maker according to the manufacturer's directions.

TO MAKE STRAWBERRY COMPOTE: Wash remaining 2 pints strawberries. Quarter larger berries and halve smaller berries. Place in a small saucepan and sprinkle with remaining ⅓ cup sugar. Let sit 15 minutes, until juices are released. Bring to a boil, then lower heat and simmer 15 minutes, or until berries are quite soft. Let cool and refrigerate until ready to use. Serve ice cream topped with compote.

Serves 6

Can you make elegant, spontaneous dessert sauces to adorn your store-bought ice cream? You bet. And the best news is that one of the ingredients is ice cream itself! Serve any of the following sauces over scoops, wedges, or disks of your favorite flavor.

Hot Fudge

⅔ **cup vanilla ice cream**

6 ounces semisweet chocolate chips, or a block of chocolate, finely chopped

2 or more tablespoons Grand Marnier

Serve this decadent sauce as soon as it is made, or reheat gently in a double boiler until molten. When cold, this sauce makes a great icing for cupcakes.

Put ice cream in a small heavy saucepan over medium heat. Let melt and then bring just to a boil. Add chocolate, then immediately lower heat. Stirring constantly, cook over very low heat until chocolate melts. Continuing to sir, add Grand Marnier, and cook 1 minute longer. Remove from heat. Serve immediately or gently reheat in a double boiler, adding a little ice cream or Grand Marnier to thin, if necessary.

Makes about 1 cup

Chocolate Sauce

1 cup vanilla ice cream

3 tablespoons cocoa powder

3 tablespoons sugar

This is surprisingly rich and chocolate-y even though it's made with cocoa powder. It's perfect at room temperature and also good slightly warmed.

Put ice cream in a small heavy saucepan. Bring just to a boil. Add cocoa powder and sugar and whisk constantly with a wire whisk. Sauce will slowly thicken. Remove from heat. If too thick, you can whisk in another tablespoon of ice cream.

Makes 1 cup

Chunky Peanut Sauce

¾ **cup sugar**

1 cup vanilla ice cream

⅓ **cup chunky or creamy
peanut butter**

*Whether you use creamy or super-chunky, everyone will love this
sauce. I think chunky is better.*

In a small heavy saucepan, put sugar and ¼ cup water. Bring to a
boil without stirring, then lower heat to medium. Continue to cook
about 10 minutes, or until liquid turns amber in color. Remove from
heat and whisk ice cream until smooth. Add a pinch of salt and the
peanut butter. Return to heat and cook 1 to 2 minutes, until smooth.
Remove from heat and let cool. Sauce will thicken, so you can add a little water or more ice cream and gently reheat as necessary.

Makes 1½ cups

Maple-Walnut Sauce

6 tablespoons pure maple syrup

½ **cup vanilla ice cream**

⅓ **heaping cup finely
chopped walnuts**

This is best served slightly warm.

In a small heavy saucepan, put maple syrup and a pinch of salt.
Bring to a boil, then lower heat to medium. Continue to cook, not stirring, about 5 minutes, until maple syrup reduces and thickens. Using
a wire whisk, whisk in ice cream and stir until completely smooth,
cooking 1 minute longer. Remove from heat and stir in walnuts. Serve
immediately or reheat gently before serving.

Makes about ½ cup

Foamy Espresso Sauce

1 cup vanilla ice cream

1 cup Marshmallow Fluff

**2 to 3 teaspoons
instant espresso powder**

*Not sure what to do with that jar of Marshmallow Fluff you've been
keeping? Here's one idea.*

In a medium nonstick skillet, melt ice cream, then bring just to a
boil. Using a wire whisk, whisk in Marshmallow Fluff and continue to
cook over low heat until fluff has melted and sauce is smooth. Whisk
in espresso powder and stir until smooth. Sauce will be a bit foamy.
Serve slightly warm or at room temperature.

Makes 1 cup

Raspberry Sauce

10 ounces frozen raspberries in sugar syrup

6 ounces fresh raspberries

6 tablespoons confectioners' sugar

Mixing fresh raspberries with frozen raspberries yields a combination of freshness and intensity neither would provide alone.

Thaw frozen raspberries and put in bowl of a food processor. Wash fresh raspberries and pat dry. Add to food processor along with confectioners' sugar and ⅓ cup water. Process until very smooth.

Place a coarse-mesh sieve over a bowl and transfer mixture to sieve. Let drain 15 minutes, then press down on the solids to extract all the liquid. Whisk in more sugar, if needed. Chill until ready to use.

Makes 1⅔ cups

Strawberry-Ginger Sauce

10 ounces frozen strawberries in syrup

2 tablespoons aromatic honey

3-inch piece fresh ginger

Here's a sauce that can jazz up almost any flavor of sorbet or ice cream. It's intensely flavored with a touch of ginger juice.

Thaw strawberries, then place them and all their liquid in bowl of a food processor. Process with ¼ cup cold water until smooth. Add honey and process until very smooth. Transfer to a coarse-mesh sieve set over a bowl and press down on the solids to extract all the liquid.

Peel ginger and grate on large holes of a box grater. Place grated ginger in a paper towel and squeeze hard to extract 2 teaspoons ginger juice, or more to taste. Stir into strawberry mixture.

Makes about 1⅔ cups

Apricot Kahlúa Sauce

½ cup sugar

½ pound dried apricots

3 tablespoons Kahlúa

This velvety thick fruit sauce is both interesting to eat and also to prepare: the secret is making a flavorful caramel "broth" in which to cook the apricots. Kahlúa, a coffee-flavored liqueur, adds a deeper layer of flavor.

In a large heavy saucepan, put sugar and cook over medium-high heat, stirring often, until sugar melts into a dark amber liquid. Carefully add 2 cups water (mixture will bubble up furiously, and sugar will harden) and continue to stir until sugar melts again and liquid is clear amber.

Add apricots and cover saucepan. Cook over medium heat about 25 minutes, until apricots are soft. Let cool 10 minutes. Transfer apricots and liquid to bowl of a food processor and process until completely smooth. Add Kahlúa and process until incorporated. Add up to ¾ cup water and process again until you have a smooth, thick, pourable sauce. Serve at room temperature or slightly warmed.

Makes 2 cups

Prune and Armagnac Sauce

2 cups prune juice

2 tablespoons honey

1 to 2 tablespoons Armagnac*

No one will ever guess what's in this magical fat-free sauce. It looks a lot like chocolate, but it's prune juice—reduced to a full-bodied syrup. Honey and Armagnac add sophistication.

Put prune juice in a small heavy saucepan and bring to a boil. Lower heat to medium and cook until reduced to ¾ cup, about 20 minutes. Whisk in honey and Armagnac and continue to cook, whisking constantly, 1 to 2 minutes. Remove from heat and let cool. Add an extra splash of Armagnac, if desired.

Makes about ¾ cup.

*You can substitute cognac.

Caramel-Rum Sauce

¾ cup vanilla-sugar

1 cup heavy cream

2 to 3 tablespoons rum

This is one of those luxurious sauces you can whip up anytime. Or keep a jar in your refrigerator at all times and gently reheat, adding another splash of rum for good measure.

Put the vanilla-sugar and ¼ cup water in a medium saucepan. Cook over medium heat, stirring constantly with a wooden spoon, until sugar dissolves and liquid is clear. Increase heat to high and cook until syrup turns a dark amber color. Remove from heat. Immediately and carefully add the cream (the mixture will bubble up), stirring constantly, until a thick, creamy caramel sauce forms. Add 2 to 3 tablespoons rum and continue to simmer 1 to 2 minutes, stirring often. Remove from heat and let cool. You can refrigerate at this point and gently warm before serving.

Makes about 1¼ cups

1-2-3 Ice Cream and Frozen Dessert Ideas

Place lemon sorbet, tiny ripe strawberries and sparkling wine in bowl of food processor. Process until thick and garnish with strawberries.

Using a melon baller, cut balls from honeydew, cantaloupe or watermelon. Splash with tequila. Layer with lime sherbet.

Fill wine glasses with raspberry sorbet and vanilla ice cream. Drizzle with Framboise (raspberry liqueur).

Coarsely chop ripe pineapple. Top with vanilla frozen yogurt and cover with coarsely chopped stem ginger in syrup.

Fill dessert coupes with chocolate ice cream. Douse with single-malt Scotch and sprinkle with finely ground hazelnut coffee beans.

Rehydrate dried apricots in apricot liqueur. Top with pistachio ice cream.

Cut a pint of coffee ice cream into wedges. Drizzle with reduced prune juice and scatter on toasted sliced almonds.

Pit fresh cherries and cook in sugar syrup. Let cool and ladle into soup plates. Top with a disk of cherry-vanilla ice cream.

Roll a ball of vanilla ice cream in toasted coconut and freeze solid. Reduce guava nectar until thick. Serve "snowball" in a puddle of guava sauce.

Make ice cream bon bons. Scoop ice cream into 1-inch balls and freeze, covered, for at least 3 hours. Melt semisweet chocolate in a double boiler. Quickly dip ice cream balls into chocolate and place on wax paper. Sprinkle with crushed nuts and refreeze.

Make ice cream bombes. Soften vanilla ice cream and two contrasting flavors and colors of sorbet. Layer each in a chilled ice cream mold, freezing each layer briefly so they maintain their separate layers. Freeze until solid. Unmold before serving.

Luxuriate with champagne sorbet. Dissolve 2 cups sugar in 2 cups boiling water. Cool and pour in large bowl. Add champagne and whipped egg white and beat until smooth. Chill and freeze in an ice cream maker according to manufacturer's directions.

A wonderful open-face ice cream sandwich from author Viana La Place: Lightly toast slices of crusty baguette and spread thickly with lemon marmalade. Using a butter knife, spread a generous layer of vanilla ice cream on top.

Try a Riesling sorbet. Process 2 pounds seedless green grapes until smooth. Strain to get 3 cups. Combine ⅓ cup sugar and 1 cup Riesling. Heat to dissolve sugar. Mix wine syrup with grape puree and freeze in an ice cream maker. Garnish with grapes.

Soften vanilla ice cream and fold in chopped candied ginger and tiny chocolate chips. Freeze until firm. Serve with chocolate sauce made from melted ice cream and chocolate chips.

Nectarine sherbet: Chop 5 very ripe nectarines and process with ¾ cup simple syrup and 1 cup milk. Strain and freeze in an ice cream maker. Remove pits from halved nectarines and mound sherbet on top of fruit. Refreeze.

Spring rhubarb ice cream: Cook 1½ pounds rhubarb in 1¼ cups water for 10 minutes. Add 1¼ cups sugar and stir. Cool. Fold in 2 cups whipped heavy cream and chill. Freeze in an ice cream maker.

Warm blueberry sundae: Top vanilla ice cream or frozen yogurt with warm blueberry syrup (page 32) whipped cream, and fresh blueberries.

Pistachio gelato: In a small saucepan put 3 cups milk and ¾ cup sugar and bring to a boil. Add 6 ounces finely ground pistachios and let sit overnight. Strain through a fine-mesh sieve and freeze in an ice cream maker.

Try exquisite honey ice cream. Heat 2 cups milk, 1 cup heavy cream and ½ cup aromatic honey–leatherwood, buckwheat, wild thyme–together and simmer several minutes until honey dissolves. Chill and then freeze in an ice cream maker.

Make chocolate ice milk by heating 3½ cup milk with 1 cup sugar and stirring into 3 ounces unsweetened melted chocolate. Chill and freeze in an ice cream maker. Garnish with chocolate shavings.

Quick sorbets: Freeze cans of fruit in syrup until frozen solid. Cut into chunks and put in bowl of food processor and process until smooth. (To make processing easier, place blade in freezer.) Splash with corresponding or complimentary liqueur and top with whipped cream sweetened with a little of the fruit's syrup: lychees with Midori; apricots with apricot liqueur; pears with Poire Williams; pineapple with dark rum; plums with plum wine; peaches with bourbon or peach schnapps.

1-2-3 parfaits: 1) lemon sorbet, crème de menthe, fresh raspberries; 2) chocolate sorbet, Irish whiskey, Marshmallow Fluff; 3) orange sorbet, Curacao, sun-dried cherries; 4) Neapolitan ice cream, strega, crushed amaretti.

What to do with a pint of ice cream: 1) Make small scoops, large scoops, quenelle-shaped scoops. 2) Place pint on its side and cut into 1½-inch-thick disks. Remove cardboard. 3) Place pint on its side and cut into 4 wedges. Remove cardboard.

Fat-Free and Low-Calorie Recipes

As with all my other 1-2-3 cookbooks, the criteria for my "healthy" categories remain stringent. To qualify as fat-free, the recipes have zero grams of fat per serving. To click into the low-calorie category, each serving has fewer than 165 calories. Enjoy all the delicious possibilities—with no sense of compromise or deprivation whatsoever.

FAT-FREE RECIPES

Strawberry-Cinnamon Compote with Melting Yogurt Timbale (if made with fat-free yogurt)
Strawberry-Lemongrass Consommé with Cut Berries
Rhubarb Compote with Candied Ginger, Maple Snow
Rhubarb-Cherry Bisque with Red Cherry Syrup
Apricot Coupe with Two Sauces (if made with fat-free pineapple cottage cheese)
Nectarine Tower with Honey-Glazed Wontons
Summer Plum and Mint Compote, Almond Sorbet
"Napoleon" of Raspberries and Oranges, Orange Sauce
Blueberries and Roasted Peaches, Fresh Blueberry Syrup
Cavaillon Melon with Glazed Cherries, Cherry Ice
Melon Tartare with Raspberries, Raspberry Coulis
Watermelon Balls in Watermelon Lemonade
Broiled Ruby Grapefruit with Mint Syrup
Pamplemousse Parisien
Grapefruit "Martini"
Cinnamon-Baked Apples with Apple Butter
Pear and Cranberry Charlotte, Cranberry Syrup
Mangoes in Sweet Lime Syrup, Lime Granita
Poached Pineapple in Lemon Syrup, Pineapple Granita
Pineapple Carpaccio with Roasted Grapes, Cinnamon Jus
Melon and Champagne Ice
Tangerine-Almond Ice with Pomegranate
Spiced Wine Granita
White Zinfandel-Raspberry Granita
Mango-Ginger Sorbet
Strawberry Sorbet with Strawberry Salad, Big Sugar Crisp
Double Raspberry Sorbet
Dessert Sauces:
    Prune and Armagnac Sauce
    Raspberry Sauce
    Apricot Kahlua Sauce
    Strawberry Ginger Sauce
    Foamy Espresso Sauce

LOW-CALORIE RECIPES

	Cal
Strawberry-Cinnamon Compote with Melting Yogurt Timbale (if made with fat-free yogurt)	161
Apricot Coupe with Two Sauces (if made with fat-free cottage cheese)	160
Melon Tartare with Raspberries, Raspberry Coulis	130
Watermelon Balls in Watermelon Lemonade	146
Pamplemousse Parisien	165
Pineapple Carpaccio and Roasted Grapes, Cinnamon Jus	165
Toasted Pecan Bars, 1 bar	165
Chickpea Flour Cookies, each	84
Moroccan Sandies, each	98
Cinnamon Shortbread, each	130
Hungarian Nut Cookies, each	96
Really Nice Sugar Cookies, each	74
Peanut Thins, each	68
Gianduia Sandwich Cookies, each	93
Ultra-Light Chocolate "Brownies"	163
Little Chocolate-Sesame Cups, each	96
Chocolate-Pepper Truffles, each	86
Pecan Fudge Terrine	120

	Cal
Chocolate Half-Moons, each	80
Granita al Caffe	165
Spiced Wine Granita	159
Mango Ginger Sorbet	165
Frosted Limes with Pepper-Lime Sorbet	138

**Dessert Sauces,
   under 55 calories per tablespoon:**

	Cal
Chocolate Sauce	34
Prune and Armagnac Sauce	50
Raspberry Sauce	22
Apricot Kahlua Sauce	33
Strawberry-Ginger Sauce	15
Foamy Espresso Sauce	53

Metric Conversion

Weight Equivalents

The metric weights given in this chart are not exact equivalents, but have been rounded up or down slightly to make measuring easier.

Avoirdupois	Metric
¼ oz	7 g
½ oz	15 g
1 oz	30 g
2 oz	60 g
3 oz	90 g
4 oz	115 g
5 oz	150 g
6 oz	175 g
7 oz	200 g
8 oz (½ lb)	225 g
9 oz	250 g
10 oz	300 g
11 oz	325 g
12 oz	350 g
13 oz	375 g
14 oz	400 g
15 oz	425 g
16 oz (1 lb)	450 g
1½ lb	750 g
2 lb	900 g
2¼ lb	1 kg
3 lb	1.4 kg
4 lb	1.8 kg

Volume Equivalents

These are not exact equivalents for American cups and spoons, but have been rounded up or down slightly to make measuring easier.

American	Metric	Imperial
¼ t	1.2 ml	
½ t	2.5 ml	
1 t	5.0 ml	
½ T (1.5 t)	7.5 ml	
1 T (3 t)	15 ml	
¼ cup (4 T)	60 ml	2 fl oz
⅓ cup (5 T)	75 ml	2½ fl oz
½ cup (8 T)	125 ml	4 fl oz
⅔ cup (10 T)	150 ml	5 fl oz
¾ cup (12 T)	175 ml	6 fl oz
1 cup (16 T)	250 ml	8 fl oz
1¼ cups	300 ml	10 fl oz (½ pt)
1½ cups	350 ml	12 fl oz
2 cups (1 pint)	500 ml	16 fl oz
2½ cups	625 ml	20 fl oz (1 pint)
1 quart	1 liter	32 fl oz

Oven Temperature Equivalents

Oven Mark	F	C	Gas
Very cool	250-275	130-140	½-1
Cool	300	150	2
Warm	325	170	3
Moderate	350	180	4
Moderately hot	375	190	5
	400	200	6
Hot	425	220	7
	450	230	8
Very hot	475	250	9